THE HOLY SPIRIT Here Today

THE HOLY SPIRIT
Here Today

formerly

CHRIST'S VICAR

by

HAROLD P. BARKER

Author of

"Christ in the Minor Prophets"
"The Three Weathervanes"
"American Stories"
"Review and Reward"
"Coming Twice"
"Royal Service"
etc.

Published by
SCRIPTURE TRUTH PUBLICATIONS
Coopies Way, Coopies Lane,
Morpeth, NE61 6JN, U.K.

Printed by
Bible Light Publishers Ltd.

Copyright © C.B.H.T. 1990
All rights reserved

ISBN 0 901860 09 3

**Printed by
Bible Light Publishers Ltd.**

CONTENTS.

	PAGE
Foreword by J. T. Mawson	11
Explanatory	13
Christ's Vicar	17
The Third Person	18
"When the Comforter is Come"	19
Sailing Ship and Steamer	21
Promise and Fact	22
"Hath"	24
"For" and "In"	25
First the Blood	27
Bought and Born	28
The Joiner and the Empty Room	29
How?	31
The Seal	32
Sealed for Security	33
When?	35
Until When?	36
Pentecost: What it was	38
Pentecost: Its Unity	39
Pentecost: The Power	41
The Four Communities	42
Seven Principal Words	44
The Baptism of the Spirit: Predictions	45
Baptised with Fire	47
Baptised into One Body	48
When were they Baptised?	50
The Actual Event	51
The Sign Gifts	53
The Abiding Presence of the Holy Spirit	54
The Comforter	56
The Helper	57
The Spirit of Truth	58
Resisting the Holy Spirit	60
Grieving the Holy Spirit	62

What Grieves Him ?	63
Bitter Memories	65
Self-Occupation	66
The Lost Chord Regained	68
Quenching the Spirit	69
Lying to the Holy Spirit	71
The Earnest	72
The Field of Clover	74
Possessed	75
Filled with the Spirit	76
Filled and Emptied	78
Shut the Gate	79
Exceptional or Normal ?	80
More of Him ?	82
The Commissioner of the Father	83
The Mission of the Servant	85
The Conductor of the Saint	88
The Controller of the Servants	89
The Compeller of the Sinner	91
Old Testament Emblems :	
(1) The Dove	92
(2) The Dew	94
(3) The Oil	95
(4) The Running Water	97
(5) The Springing Well	98
The Seven Spirits of God	99
(1) The Spirit of Creative Energy	101
(2) The Spirit of Restraint	102
(3) The Spirit of Prophecy and Inspiration	104
(4) The Spirit of Holiness	105
(5) The Spirit of Grace	107
(6) The Spirit of Judgment	108
(7) The Spirit of Earthwide Blessing	109
The Laying on of Hands	109
"Have Ye Received the Holy Ghost ?"	111

The Witness	112
(1) What is it?	114
(2) A Common Mistake	115
(3) A Mistake Corrected	117
(4) The Person and His Testimony	118
(5) Nothing Mysterious	120
(6) "To" and "With"	121
(7) "With Our Spirit"	123
(8) Eternal Life	124
(9) A Few More Words	126
The Christian's Body	127
Blaspheming against the Holy Spirit	128
The Backslider and the Unpardonable Sin	130
"If They Shall Fall Away"	132
"Partakers of the Holy Ghost"	133
Access by One Spirit	135
An Habitation of God through the Spirit	136
Strengthened with Might by His Spirit	137
The Fruit of the Spirit	139
The Spirit of Life in Christ Jesus	140
The Spirit of Sonship	141
The Cross and the Spirit	143
The Spirit's Day	144
More Great Things	146
The Heiress and the Key	148
The Holy Spirit and the World	149
The Holy Spirit and Hymns	150
The Unction	160
The Winning Side	161
Worshipping by the Spirit	163
New Testament Principles	165
Montanists and Others	166
The Hope of Righteousness	168
The Spirit of Jesus	170
First and Last Mentions	171
The Benediction	173
A Warning	174
Index of Texts	177

"The Spirit, ministering these things to us, glorifying Christ . . . being HIS VICAR and Substitute upon earth."
—*Darby.*

*   *   *   *

"Praises for the Holy Ghost,
    Sent from heaven at Pentecost;
    'Tis through Him alone we live
    And the precious truth receive."
—*Montgomery.*

*   *   *   *

(Deep) "secrets, which were veiled of yore,
And angels study more and more,
The infant scholars of the Spirit learn."
—*Montgomery.*

FOREWORD.

By J. T. Mawson.

A well-known Christian teacher once threw out a challenge to preachers of the Gospel. He asked: "If you were sent with three or four great benefits to a sick person, would you be justified in giving him only one of these, because it afforded him some relief, and withholding the others ? Surely not ; for by so doing you would be guilty of a double injustice. You would not rightly represent the kindness of the donor, and you would be withholding from the sufferer what was intended for his good."

He was speaking of the forgiveness of sins, an inestimable boon. Blessed is the man who has received it ! And what he sought to show was that along with it God gives His Holy Spirit. He urged upon gospel preachers that they were responsible to tell their hearers this.

He was right, as the whole of the New Testament proves. Think of the man whose limbs were shaking with an incurable palsy, and who, through the persistent kindness and faith of his four friends, lay looking up into the face of the Lord Jesus. How his heart must have thrilled as he heard those peace-giving words : " Thy sins are forgiven thee." Poor fellow ! What a burden those sins had been to his soul ! And now, from the lips of incarnate Truth the word of relief is uttered. But was that all ? Indeed, no ; the pardoned sinner was to become the empowered saint, glorifying God by his walk.

Think again of that matchless parable of the good Samaritan who succoured the stricken man on the Jericho road. The oil and the wine were comforting and healing as they were poured into his wounds. How tender were the hands that bound up those wounds! But was that all? No; "he put him on his own beast." He cured him, certainly, but he *carried* him, too. His power was placed at his disposal.

The miracle and the parable in the Gospels teach the same lesson that the Acts and the Epistles demonstrate, that when God pardons a man for Christ's sake, He gives him the Spirit, the power of a new life.

No subject therefore can be of greater importance to the pardoned sinner than that of the Holy Spirit. His capacity to understand the things of God, his power for Christian living and service, the means by which he may commune with God and intercede with Him on behalf of others are all found in the Holy Spirit "whom God hath given to them that obey Him."

God grant that every reader of this book may gain an enlarged conception of the greatness and necessity of this gift, and increased appreciation of it, and a deeper sense of the holiness that should be one of the chief features of those in whom the Holy Spirit dwells, that they grieve Him not, nor hinder His gracious work in them and through them.

EXPLANATORY.

Dr. Elder Cumming gives, as a reason for the writing of his volume on the Holy Spirit, the fact that in the treatises of his predecessors " there has not always been an adherence to a definite method, proceeding from step to step, either in the order of revelation or in the order of thought."

Whatever would the good doctor have said of this book ? Probably he would have repeated his criticism in intensified form. But the Scriptures do not codify truth. We find it interwoven with history, introduced incidentally, clothed with the language of poetry, dealt with in informal letters, and but rarely taught in what we moderns would call a systematic manner.

This book follows the more Scriptural plan. Yet it is not put together in a haphazard fashion. The reader will discern a certain order, that which is fundamental receiving priority of treatment. In dealing with such a tremendous theme much, of course, must be omitted. I have kept in mind what Professor Saintsbury said to one Phrynichus. He was, we are told, "redundant and garrulous ; for when it was open to him to have got the matter completely finished off in not a fifth part of his actual length, by saying things out of season he has stretched his matter out to an unmanageable bulk."

People like Phrynichus defeat their own aims. Their writings go unread. Hence the brevity of the following chapters. Under each heading much more might have been said. The subjects lend themselves to fuller treatment. But a large extent of ground has been covered, as the index of texts shows.

That another book on the subject of the Holy Spirit should be added to the already large number, calls for a few words of explanation. I have read many of these books. Some are stodgy, some are scrappy, some are too doctrinal, some are not doctrinal enough, some are misleading, and some are admirable. We know not what adjective our friends will use to describe this volume, but they will admit that it covers most of the ground and is divided into short, readable chapters.

In the worship of that strange and somewhat unwholesome sect of Russian origin, the Doukhobors, a point comes when all present rise and make profound bows one to another. It is their way of acknowledging the truth that the Holy Spirit indwells the body of each believer. It is to Him that they make their obeisance. I am not suggesting that this custom should be adopted by others, but anything is better than to ignore the fact of the Holy Spirit's presence.

The two great outstanding facts of the present time, which make Christianity what it is, are (1) that a MAN sits at the right hand of God in heaven, and (2) that the Third Person of the Godhead is a Resident upon this planet.

If this book conveys no information, and unfolds nothing concerning the Holy Spirit that is not already known, it will at least justify its existence if it calls attention once again to the truth that the One who came at Pentecost has never since departed. That the hour when His residence will terminate seems to be not far off lends greater urgency to the fact.

In the case of passages regarded as " difficult," I have sought to expound them as profitable and necessary rather than to explain them away as hard to fit in with received evangelical doctrine. To point out what a passage does *not* mean may sometimes be helpful. But to unfold it as containing necessary truth is a thousand times more so.

Above all, knowledge as a basis of devotion and of action, rather than a mere accretion of Biblical information, has been my aim. The book is written not so much with a desire that instruction may be given as to the Person and Work of the Holy Spirit, as that increasingly He may be a power in the lives of Christian readers, and that they may be induced more and more to give Him right of way in their outlook, their decisions, their motives, their affections and their desires.

CHRIST'S VICAR

" Christ has His representative on earth to-day, and I am happy to belong to that holy and apostolic Church over which the Vicar of Christ presides."

So said an ardent advocate of Roman Catholicism. If only the words had been spoken in a different connection they would have expressed a great truth. But, of course, the Romanist was speaking of his Pope, while his words can only be true when used of the Holy Spirit. For the Holy Spirit is indeed Christ's Representative and Vicar on earth.

When the Lord, at the close of His sojourn on earth, was about to return to heaven, He spoke of "another Comforter" who should come to dwell in those who belong to Him (John xiv. 16). This Comforter, the Holy Spirit, would be sent from God the Father *in Christ's Name* (John xiv. 26), that is, as the Representative of Christ, to do His work, care for His interests, and act on His behalf. He would be the divine Plenipotentiary, not speaking of (that is, from) Himself, but receiving the things of Christ and showing them to the men who are called by His Name (John xvi. 14).

The Holy Spirit has not come to bear witness to Himself. In wonderful grace He has come as the Divine Servant of the Godhead. His ministry is to attract men to Christ.

I once saw in a Canadian paper a cartoon that much impressed me. A single human hand was grasping a loaf of bread and holding it towards a crowd of men and women. The loaf was inscribed "Christ," the hand "the Church," and under the picture were the words: "All she has to offer." How true! This is the situation exactly. Whether by the Church, or by an individual Christian, or by means of a silent, printed page, all that the Holy Spirit has to offer may be summed up in the one word: CHRIST.

In olden times He bore witness through a long line of prophets of the Christ that was to come (Acts x. 43). Now, in a more personal way, He testifies of the Christ that is seated as Man at the right hand of God.

THE THIRD PERSON.

When the Lord Jesus Christ was on earth He was "Emmanuel, which being interpreted is, God with us." (Matthew i. 23). The second Person of the Divine Trinity made God visible to men. He dwelt for years among them and they beheld His glory.

Not one whit less true is it that in our day also there is a Divine Person on earth, dwelling here in and with the children of God. He is not the second, but the third Person of the Triune Godhead. No body has been prepared for Him. A body was prepared for Christ (Hebrews x. 5), but the Holy Spirit has not become incarnate. He dwells in the bodies of believers; these bodies of ours are the temples wherein He manifests Himself (I Corinthians vi. 19).

Let us have it clearly before our minds that He is as truly a Person as Christ is. We cannot see Him, but His personality and presence are facts.

We say this because many seem to have an idea that He is a kind of influence emanating from God, and they invariably speak of Him as " it." Needless to say, He *exerts* a great and blessed influence, but He Himself is more than an influence. He wields wonderful power, but He Himself is more than a power.

This is plainly shown in John xvi. 13, 14. In these two verses seven things are stated which prove Him, beyond all doubt, to be a real Person. See what they are : (1) He comes ; (2) He guides ; (3) He hears ; (4) He speaks ; (5) He glorifies ; (6) He receives ; (7) He shows. Some of these things might be predicated of a power or an influence, but not all. Can a power hear ? Can an influence receive ? Of course not. These seven things prove that the One who does them is indeed a Person.

Another Scripture tells us that He may be grieved (Ephesians iv. 30). Can a power or an influence be grieved ?

Notice, moreover, that in the two verses from John xvi. referred to above, the pronoun " He " is used eight times. We do not speak of an influence or of a power as " He." But when we refer to the Holy Spirit we say " He."

" WHEN THE COMFORTER IS COME."

These words, quoted from John xv. 26, show that at the time when they were uttered, the Holy Spirit had not come. This is clearly the force also of the words in John xvi. 13 : " When He, the Spirit of truth, is come." Such words may well be used of anyone who is expected in a place, but would have no meaning if the person were already there.

I may be reminded, however, that we read of the Holy Spirit's work in the world in times that preceded the coming of Christ. Did He not at the very beginning move upon the face of the waters ? Was He not with David when he prayed : " Take not Thy Holy Spirit from me ? " Did He not come upon chosen vessels from time to time : men like Bezaleel, Gideon and others ?

All this, of course, is true. But it is evident that the Lord had something different in view when He said : " When the Comforter is come." Something entirely new was before His mind when He spoke in this fashion. Nor is this the only instance where the coming of the Holy Spirit is referred to in the Gospels as a future event. In John xiv. 16, the Lord Jesus said to His disciples : " I will pray the Father and He *shall give you* another Comforter." So too in verse 26 : " the Holy Ghost, whom the Father *will send.*"

The explanation of this is very simple. While writing these lines I am staying for a few weeks in Trinidad. It is the third time I have been here, but never otherwise than as a visitor. Let us suppose that it is my intention to buy a house and take up my residence in the island.

In conversation with a friend, I happen to speak of something which I hope to do " when I come to Trinidad.''

My friend looks at me with surprise. " What do you mean by saying ' when I come to Trinidad ' ? " he enquires ; " You are here now, and have been before."

" True," I reply, " but have you not heard that I am coming to Trinidad in a new way ? I have been here these three times *as a visitor*, but I hope shortly to come and make my abode here."

In this way we are to understand Christ's words when He spoke of the coming of the Comforter. He had been to earth many times, but only as a Visitor. He was soon to come as a Resident, to *abide for ever* with those to whom He should be given.

SAILING SHIP AND STEAMER.

It was not only because the Holy Spirit was to *abide* that His promised coming was to differ from all that had gone before.

In the former days the occasions of His coming were, for the most part, to endue with power some chosen instrument for a particular purpose. Hence we generally read that He came *on* the subjects of His visitation. He came on Othniel, on Gideon, on Jephthah, on Samson, on David, on Azariah, on Jahaziel, on Zechariah, and so forth.

In contrast with this, Christ said, in John xiv. 17: "He shall be *in* you." And Paul writes to the believers at Corinth of "the Holy Ghost which is *in* you" (I Corinthians vi. 19). Elsewhere he speaks of "His Spirit that dwelleth *in* you" (Rom. viii. 11) and of "the Holy Ghost which dwelleth *in* us" (II Timothy i. 14).

The importance of the distinction between ON and IN is greater than one would at first suppose. By way of illustration, think of the contrast between an old-fashioned sailing vessel and a modern steamer. The sailing vessel is dependent for its progress on *a power coming upon it* from without. When the wind fills its sails progress is easy and rapid. The steamship, on the other hand, is driven by a *power within*, a power which is not intermittent, but constant. The wind may blow, the waves may run mountains high, but all the time the steamer ploughs her way onward, because the power that drives her is *within*.

In the day before Christ came God's people were like the sailing vessel. To-day they are like the steamer. Our progress is dependent on a power within, and not our progress only, but our joy, our service, our testimony, all depend upon the *indwelling* and abiding Comforter. Without Him, and His gracious work in our souls, there can be no true knowledge of God, nor understanding of His great things.

Even upon men who were not men of God at all the Holy Spirit came, to bend them and use them for His purpose. He came upon that evil man Balaam, and upon Saul, who eventually died under God's displeasure. But He never *indwells* such. Only to those who are redeemed by the precious blood of Christ does He come to-day. "The world cannot receive" Him, said our Lord, "because it seeth Him not, neither knoweth Him." But, He adds, "He dwelleth with *you*, and shall be in *you*" (John xiv. 17).

PROMISE AND FACT.

It is one of the greatest, most fundamental, most significant, most characteristic, most far-reaching truths of Christianity that the Third Person of the Godhead is Resident upon this planet that we call the Earth.

Before, however, He could come to take up His abode here, a certain event had to take place. This is clearly stated in John vii. 39: "This spake He of the Spirit,

THE HOLY SPIRIT Here Today 23

which they that believe on Him should receive, for the Holy Ghost was not yet given, because that *Jesus was not yet glorified.*"

The exaltation of the rejected Jesus must take place before the Holy Spirit could be given in the new and wonderful way promised by our Lord. Hence He says: "*If I go not away*, the Comforter will not come unto you; but if I depart, I will send Him unto you" (John xvi.7).

At length the time arrived for the fulfilment of the promise. The long-expected Comforter was sent. Full details of His coming are given in Acts ii.

Before His coming, the Lord taught His disciples, as in Luke xi. 13, to pray for the Holy Spirit. No doubt it was for His coming that the one hundred and twenty "all continued with one accord in prayer and supplication" (Acts i. 14). But at last prayer gave place to praise. The earth-rejected Jesus had been glorified in heaven and, "being by the right hand of God exalted," He sent the Holy Spirit to dwell in His people, and to abide with them for ever.

From that moment onward we search in vain for any such thing as *asking for the Holy Spirit*. Right and proper as such a prayer would be before His coming, it would be out of place now that He has been given. For a Christian, living during the present time of the Comforter's presence on earth, to pray as those who lived before His coming prayed, is to pray the prayer either of ignorance or of unbelief.

We may and should pray to be kept from grieving Him; that we may be strengthened with might by the Spirit in the inner man; that He may fill us, so that rivers of living water may flow out to others from us as the channels; that we may be divinely aided in our endeavours to keep the unity of the Spirit in the bond of peace ; and that we may abound in hope through the power of the Holy Spirit. For all such things it is right that we should continually pray.

But all this is very different from praying that the Holy Spirit may be given to us. Rather let us give thanks to God for this great gift that He has bestowed on us.

" HATH."

Let me ask the reader a question. Would it be right for a real believer in Christ to pray for the forgiveness of all his sins ?

" Assuredly not," you reply, " for we read that God, for Christ's sake, HATH forgiven us " (Eph. iv. 32).

Would it be right for him to pray for the gift of everlasting life ?

" Certainly not," you say, " for ' he that believeth on the Son HATH everlasting life.' It would not be intelligent for one to pray for what is already his."

You would say the same if I enquired as to whether we should pray for other blessings, such as meetness for heaven. For we read of " giving thanks to the Father, which HATH made us meet to be partakers of the inheritance of the saints in light" (Colossians i. 12).

All this is very clear. Now let us point out that the same golden word " hath " is used more than once in the New Testament in connection with the gift of the Holy Spirit.

We read of " the Holy Ghost, whom God HATH given to them that obey Him " (Acts v. 32). In II Corinthians i. 22 we are told that God " HATH also sealed us, and given us the earnest of the Spirit in our hearts." Also, in Galatians iv. 6 : " because ye are sons, God HATH sent forth the Spirit of His Son into your hearts " ; in I Thessalonians iv. 8 : " God, who HATH also given unto us His Holy Spirit " ; and in I John iii. 24 : " the Spirit which He HATH given us."

These passages show that the gift of the Holy Spirit, instead of being a matter for prayer, is, for the Christian, a subject of praise and thanksgiving.

As someone has remarked, " God's forgiving and giving go together." He forgives our sins and gives us His Holy Spirit. The two things, the forgiveness and the gift, are coupled together by Peter in Acts ii. 38. He declared to his hearers that the remission of sins should be accompanied by the gift of the Holy Spirit.

If you have never gratefully and sincerely thanked God your Father for this tremendous gift, will you do so this very day ? Let it be the first of many such thanksgivings.

" FOR " AND " IN."

We do indeed, read of prayer in connection with the Holy Spirit, but not (in this Christian era) of prayer *for* Him. On the contrary, we are exhorted to make " prayer and supplication *in* the Spirit " and to be " praying *in* the Holy Ghost " (Ephesians vi. 18 ; Jude 20).

The difference between praying *for* and praying *in* the Holy Spirit is not difficult to see. But the following illustration will make it quite clear.

A Christian friend was very anxious that the writer

should bring his large Gospel Tent to the village where he lived.

"You can pitch it on the lawn in front of my house," he said, "and I hope and pray that you may be led to bring it and have meetings in it."

"Very well," I replied, "go on praying for it ; it is the best way to bring to pass what you desire."

So for several weeks my friend continued in prayer that God would direct that the Tent should be brought to his village.

At last the way was open, and the Tent was taken there and pitched. The poles and canvas were put up, the seats arranged and dusted, and the lamps hung in their places.

"Now," said the Christian brother, "before we go to my house and have some tea, let us kneel down and ask God's blessing on the meetings to be held here.

So we knelt down, and the first voice to be raised in prayer was that of my good friend.

Surely anyone can see the difference between this Christian man praying FOR the Tent to be brought, and then praying IN the Tent after it had come. Just as simple is the difference between praying *for* the Holy Spirit, so right and suitable in the days before He came, and praying *in* the Holy Spirit in this, the day of His residence on earth.

Instead of beseeching God to pour out His Spirit upon us, we have to thank Him for the gift of the Comforter, and to let our prayers be the expression of desires which He has wrought in our souls.

FIRST THE BLOOD.

It may be objected by one who reads the foregoing chapter, and is not well grounded in the teaching of the Scriptures, that since the Holy Spirit is not given to everybody, it cannot be wrong for those who have not received Him to pray for this great gift.

But for an unregenerate man to pray for the Holy Spirit is to pray for something that God will not and cannot grant. He never gives His Spirit to unbelievers. They are part of that world which the Lord declared was unable to receive Him (John xiv. 17). Something must take place first.

An illustration from the Old Testament will help us here. In the ritual prescribed in connection with the cleansing of the leper in Leviticus xiv. the priest had first to apply *the blood* of a lamb to the ear, the thumb and the great toe of the man. Having done this he had to put some *oil* on the ear, the thumb and the great toe (verses 14 and 17).

Note the order : first the blood, then the oil. Now oil is frequently used in the Bible as an emblem of the Holy Spirit. The type teaches us that His indwelling can only take place where the blood has been applied.

It is useless for an unconverted man to pray for the Holy Spirit. What such a man needs is cleansing by the precious blood of Christ through faith in Him as Saviour. He need not even then pray for the Holy Spirit, for when he believes unto salvation God will surely seal him with the Holy Spirit.

It is not merely to ripe and advanced believers that He is given, but to *all* who put their trust in the Saviour and believe the gospel of their salvation. It is not their worthiness, their service, their personal holiness or their intelligence that entitles them to receive this great gift. Their title lies in the precious blood of Christ. Where cleansing and redemption through His blood have been received, there the Holy Spirit can and does take up His abode.

BOUGHT AND BORN.

There is another necessary lesson that we may learn from the ancient ritual ordained by God for the people of Israel. We read in Leviticus xxii. 10, 11 that certain people had neither part nor lot in the things that were hallowed unto the Lord. (1) The stranger, (2) the sojourner, and (3) the hired servant might not participate. Only one (1) *bought* by the priest, or (2) *born* in his house might " eat of the holy thing."

For any of us to have the salvation of God it is not a matter of being bought *or* born. We have to be both bought *and* born ; bought with the blood of Christ and born of the Spirit (John iii. 6).

In the language of Scripture the unregenerate man is only " flesh," and in order that he may be led into the paths of true blessing and righteousness he must be born again (John iii. 3). When this takes place there is a new principle of being, a new life and nature within, which had no existence there before. This is what the Lord referred to when He said : " that which is born of the Spirit is spirit." It is connection with this new life and nature, and not the " flesh," that the Holy Spirit subsequently works.

It is very important that we should be clear as to this, and a simple illustration may serve to make it plain.

In a certain place stood a hall where some Christians

were wont to meet for worship. In course of time it became too small, and it was resolved to pull it down and build another. The writer happened to be in the locality while the building was in progress. One morning, in company with his kind host, who had charge of the operations, he strolled round to see how it was getting on.

"This must be a costly undertaking," he remarked.

"Not quite so much as you would think," was the reply, "for, you see, we are *using a lot of the old material for the new building.*"

Now this is exactly what the Holy Spirit cannot do. He cannot use one particle of "the flesh," the old material which God has condemned. If He is to carry on a work in anyone's soul, leading him to know God and enter into the enjoyment of the blessings of Christianity, He must begin by implanting a new life and nature. It is this that is effected in the new birth.

THE JOINER AND THE EMPTY ROOM.

Someone has tritely and truly remarked that "the Holy Spirit has a great deal more to do IN us than He has to do THROUGH us." However much He may be pleased to use us in the service of Christ, the most important thing is that His work in our own souls should prosper.

As we have shown in the preceding chapter, the new birth is the beginning of the work of the Holy Spirit in the soul of the believer. It is the creation of the material upon which He can subsequently work.

Let us suppose that a joiner, one of the most skilful of his trade, is taken to an empty room. He has with him a case of the best and most up-to-date tools. He is required to make a table and to remain in the room till it is made.

" But," he exclaims, " you demand what is impossible. There is no material here on which I can work. I must have wood if I am to make a table."

It is the same with the Holy Spirit. Before He can do His work in us He must have suitable material. This is why we *must* be born again. Apart from the new birth there is no material in us that He can use to produce what He desires. He cannot work on our natural emotions nor on the most refined feelings. He can only work upon the material that He produces within us when we are born again.

What is the work which the Holy Spirit seeks to do in the souls of believers? It is that of which Paul speaks in Galatians iv. 19. He labours to *form Christ* in us. That is, He works to displace the old motives, desires and inclinations and to make Christ the centre of our affections and aims, so that He may be reproduced in our lives and seen in our actions.

The Galatian believers, like all others of whom we read in the New Testament, had by their baptism " put on " Christ (Galatians iii. 27). That is, their baptism unto Christ had been their public avowal of their faith in Him. But something further was needed, and for this the apostle travailed in birth again, as it were. It was that Christ might be formed IN them, dwelling in their affections and manifesting Himself in their lives.

HOW ?

If the question be asked, " *How* is a man born again ? ' we can only reply that it is by the sovereign action of the Spirit of God using the " water " as the means. But as to the precise manner of the operation, Scripture likens Him to the wind which blows where it lists. The *result* is perceived, but whence it comes and whither it goes none can tell (John iii. 8).

We are " born of water and of the Spirit " (John iii. 5). To understand the significance of " water " in this passage one needs to be intelligent as to the use of symbols in Scripture. Otherwise one may fall into the error of the ritualist, who deduces baptismal regeneration from this verse.

In the Gospel of John " water " has often a symbolic meaning. When the Lord spoke of the water that He gives, and the well of water within (iv. 14); when He promised that when the Holy Spirit came " rivers of living water " should flow out from those who believe (vii. 38); no one imagines that He meant real water, the substance known to chemists as H_2O.

We are not left without a clue to the spiritual significance of water as one of the agencies by which the new birth is effected. We read in James i. 18 that God begat us with *the word of truth*. And in I Peter i. 23 we are told that we have been born again *by the word of God*. " And this is the word," adds the apostle in verse 25, " which by the gospel is preached unto you."

The " water " then is manifestly a symbol of the Word of God. Effectually applied by the Holy Spirit, it is the instrument by which the new birth is brought to pass. This is confirmed by Ephesians v. 26 where, in another connection, we read of " the washing of water *by the word*."

As in creation the word and the Spirit wrought to produce the heavens and the earth, so it is in the new birth. *God said* " Let there be light." That was the word. " and there was light." That is, the Spirit who moved on the face of the waters wrought in accord with the word. Again : " God said, Let there be a firmament." That was His word. " And God made the firmament." By His Spirit He wrought to give effect to His word.

Even so is it in connection with the new birth.

THE SEAL.

Three times in the New Testament we read of our being sealed with the Holy Spirit. It is not that the Holy Spirit seals us, but that He IS the Seal by which we are marked as belonging to Christ. It is God " who hath also sealed us " (II Corinthians i. 22). We are marked as Christ's, not by being branded in the forehead, not by being bidden to wear a peculiar dress, but by having the Holy Spirit to indwell us.

We must be careful not to confound being born of the Spirit with being sealed. The two things are quite different. We are born of the Spirit *in order that we may be* the children of God. We are sealed with the Spirit *because we are* His children, and belong to Christ.

A farmer goes to market and buys some sheep. " Now," says he, " I will brand them with the initial letter of my name, so that if any should stray, I shall be able to recognize them as mine."

Having paid the price, he proceeds to mark them.

The branding does not make them his ; the purchase money did that. He marks them *because they are his.*

Or again, I go to a shop and buy some collars. When I get home I take my bottle of marking ink and mark them in the corner with my name. Why do I do this ? Not to make the collars mine. The price that I paid for them made them my property. I mark them because I want them to be *known as mine*, whether in the laundry or wherever they may be found.

With the believer it is the same. Bought with the precious blood of Christ, he now belongs to Him. And because of this, God seals him by giving him the Holy Spirit to dwell within him. We are thus " sealed with that Holy Spirit of Promise " (Eph. i. 13).

On what ground are we sealed? Let us make no mistake as to this. The Lord Jesus, when He was here, was sealed by God the Father (John vi. 27). This was on the ground of His own personal perfection. But with us it is different. The Holy Spirit is not given to us because of anything that we are in ourselves. We are not sealed because of our sanctity, our progress, our maturity or our devotion. We are sealed simply and solely because we have been redeemed with the precious blood of Christ. We are sealed because we stand in all the abiding efficacy of His once offered sacrifice.

SEALED FOR SECURITY.

A leading thought connected with sealing in Scripture is that of security. A thing was sealed to make it secure for its owner.

An interesting thing is often seen in a market in

Morocco. A man buys some sacks of corn, and immediately proceeds to seal them. Having sealed them as his property, he goes for his donkey. Then he returns to the market, claims the sacks of corn that he has sealed, and carries them off.

It is the same with us. God has sealed us, leaving us here for a while, until Christ comes to fetch us away.

The chief priests and Pharisees came to the Roman governor after the Lord had been crucified and buried, saying, " Sir, we remember that that deceiver said, while He was yet alive, ' After three days I will rise again.' Command therefore that the sepulchre *be made sure* until the third day, lest His disciples come by night and steal Him away and say unto the people, ' He is risen from the dead.' "

Mark the governor's reply. It looks as if he were tired of those crafty men, and would not go further out of his way to oblige them.

" Ye have a watch," he says, " go your way, *make it as sure as ye can.*"

Observe how they did this. Their object was to make the sepulchre absolutely sure, lest it should be despoiled of its contents : " So they went and made the sepulchre sure, sealing the stone, and setting a watch " (Matthew xxvii. 66).

By these two things they sought to make the sepulchre sure, as sure as they could: (1) by sealing it; (2) by setting a watch. And in similar ways God has made us *as sure as He can* :   (1) by sealing us with the Holy Spirit, and (2) by setting a watch over us, for " He withdraweth not His eyes from the righteous " (Job xxxvi. 7). He watches over us by day and by night.

Was the sepulchre made sure by those priests and Pharisees ? No ; for a greater power than theirs broke their seal, overpowered the watchers, and robbed the tomb of its contents. Can any such thing happen to those whom God has sealed with the Holy Spirit ? Thank God, no ; there is no power in the universe that can break His seal or imperil those whom He has placed in safety. He has made us *as sure as He can* ! Our security is absolute.

WHEN ?

Exactly when does the believer receive the Holy Spirit ? Is it at the moment of his conversion, or at some subsequent period of his Christian life ?

Turn to the Epistle to the Romans. Chapters iii and iv unfold the way of justification for ungodly sinners. At the beginning of Chapter v we arrive at the point that being justified by faith we have peace with God. And His love is shed abroad in our hearts (verse 5). By what means ? " By the Holy Ghost which is given unto us." We conclude that justification by faith is accompanied by the gift of the Holy Spirit.

An objection to this is based on the words of Ephesians i. 13 : " *after* that ye believed, ye were sealed." But there is no thought of chronological sequence in the verse. We should read preferably " on believing, ye were sealed." The sequence is a moral, not a chronological one. When a wheel begins to turn round, one spoke follows another, but no spoke starts moving before the others. You may number them 1, 2, 3 and so on, and observe that one always follows the others in this order. But they all start moving at the same moment. There is no interval of time between No. 1 starting and No. 2 starting, though No. 2 follows No. 1.

Thus it is with the believer. Call believing, Spoke No. 1 ; justification, Spoke No. 2 ; the gift of the Holy Spirit, Spoke No. 3. They go in this order, but as far as *time* is concerned all coincide.

There were exceptions to this general rule in the days of transition of which we read in the Acts. These are explained in pages 80 to 83. But in Acts x we find the principle on which believers, especially those from among the Gentiles, receive the Holy Spirit. Peter was preaching in the house of Cornelius. He came to these words : " whosoever believeth in Him shall receive remission of sins " (verse 43). Those who listened were evidently mixing what they heard with faith. They received the glad tidings, and while Peter was still speaking " the Holy Ghost fell on all them which heard the word." There was no interval, no waiting, no laying on of hands. Hearing, believing and receiving the Holy Spirit all went together.

UNTIL WHEN ?

Until when are we sealed with the Holy Spirit ? Some will say, " Until we grieve Him away." But Scripture gives a very different answer. " Ye are sealed." we read, " *until the day of redemption* " (Ephesians iv. 30).

Needless to say, this cannot refer to the day of the *soul's* redemption, for that day has already dawned for every believer in Christ. But there is a redemption still future, for which we wait. " Waiting for the adoption, to wit, the redemption of *our body* " (Romans viii. 23).

Our bodies are not yet redeemed though they belong to Christ and are indwelt by the Holy Spirit. They are still liable to decay and death. But the day is coming when they will be redeemed from the last trace of Adam's likeness and made just like Christ's own body of glory. This is the redemption for which we are still waiting, and it is drawing nearer all the time.

It is upon this fact that the exhortation not to grieve the Holy Spirit is based. If we *do* grieve Him, He will not leave us, but will withhold from us that joy and comfort which He otherwise delights to give. In this way we are made to feel how serious a thing it is to grieve Him.

" But," says someone, " I knew a man under deep religious conviction. The Holy Spirit was evidently striving with him, but the man resisted, and resumed his old ways, more hardened than ever. Does not such an experience refute the assertion that when the Holy Spirit takes up His abode in a man, He does so for ever, and never withdraws ? "

By no means. It is true that the Holy Spirit strives with sinners and that His strivings may be resisted. It may be that when this is the case He sometimes ceases to strive, and never again does the sinner feel any real desire for salvation.

This, however, is an entirely different matter from that of which we have been speaking. Who does not see the difference between a man building a house and then going to live in it when it has been built ? Equally clear is the difference between the Holy Spirit striving with a man in order to lead him to repentance and faith in the Saviour, and His taking up His abode in that man when he believes.

When one believes the Gospel and is, in consequence, sealed with the Holy Spirit, he is sealed "unto the day of redemption." But of this we shall have more to say in the chapter on Grieving the Spirit. We must first devote a few pages to an explanation of what took place on the Day of Pentecost.

PENTECOST : WHAT IT WAS.

There are persons to-day, some of them of decided spiritual excellence, whose slogan seems to be "Back to Pentecost." They are continually exhorting folks to seek pentecostal blessing, pentecostal fire, pentecostal power, and so forth. It will be well, therefore, carefully to enquire what Pentecost really was.

Three things stand out prominently. They are what made the great event of the Coming of the Holy Spirit at Pentecost so tremendously significant.

(1) Pentecost was the INAUGURATION OF A NEW THING ON THE EARTH. It was the beginning of Christianity. It was the birthday of the Church.

When the magnificent tunnel under the Mersey was completed, no less a person than His Majesty the King, accompanied by the Queen, went to open it. The inauguration has never had to be repeated, but from that day the tunnel has remained open for use.

When in the ways of God the new thing that He had purposed to bring to pass was to be established, the Holy Spirit Himself came to inaugurate it. The inauguration has never had to be repeated. There has been no second Pentecost. How could there be ? Can a thing be brought into being more than once ? A bell rings to announce that the service is about to begin. When the service has begun, does the bell continue ringing?

Speaking with tongues and other miraculous happenings were the manifest authentication of this new thing, Christianity, as being of divine origin. They bore witness to the fact of a Divine Person having come. What need is there for their continuance or their repetition?

An important document has to be duly attested. The witnesses sign their names and perhaps affix their seals. It is sufficient that they do this *once for all*. Their signatures have not to be repeated; they have not to affix their seals again and again.

Similarly, those who are intelligent as to what Pentecost really meant will not look for a repetition to-day. They are content to know that the thing of which they are a part was started on its course here on earth by marks of divine authentication as the Holy Spirit came to bring it into being.

PENTECOST: ITS UNITY.

(2) One hundred and twenty people went up the stairs to that upper room on the memorable day of which we read in Acts ii, and *one* came down. I do not say that one *person* came down; as many came down as went up. But in the upper room something had happened that had welded them into a corporate whole, the One Body of Christ.

In the olden days those that feared the Lord sometimes got very close to one another, and " spake often one to to another." But there was no organic link between them. They were like apples in a barrel, pressed tightly together but with no union between the different apples. If the barrel be emptied out, the apples go rolling in all directions. Nothing binds them together in one.

In Christianity the human body is used as a figure to set forth the relations of Christians one with another. We are fellow-members of one Body! Now if a man falls down in the street, his fingers and feet, his eyes and ears, do not go rolling away as the apples when tipped out of the barrel. They are united one with another, being parts of an organism.

It is the same with us Christians. We are not like those who lived under the old economy. *They* were like the apples : *we* are members of a living organism, formed at Pentecost, when the Holy Spirit was given to each of those assembled. Being indwelt by the one Spirit, we together form the one Body.

And this, let me repeat, is not an organisation, but an organism. A Horticultural Society is an organization. It has its President, its Vice-President, its Secretary, its Treasurer, and its Committee of control. But an *organism* is not constituted like that. The human body is not governed by a President, Secretary, Treasurer and Committee of control ! It is governed by a head.

Even so is it with the Body of Christ. It is guided and governed by its Head, and its members are left on earth that the graces of the Head might be reproduced in them.

May God grant that the great truth of the unity that came into being at Pentecost may colour our lives increasingly, and make us always ready to recognize every Christian (even if we only meet him casually in a train or bus) as a fellow-member of Christ's body, one with ourselves in Him. In this way we may endeavour " to keep the unity of the Spirit in the bond of peace " (Ephesians iv. 3).

PENTECOST : THE POWER.

(3) The third outstanding feature of Pentecost was that the servants of Christ were then equipped with a new and wonderful *power*. " Ye shall receive power, after that the Holy Ghost is come upon you," said the risen Christ (Acts i. 8) ; and He bade them " tarry ye in the city of Jerusalem until ye be endued with power from on high " (Luke xxiv. 49).

The power that was to make their witness to Christ effective was not to be that of *the sword*. It was left to Mohammed and his successors to make proselytes by threats of death. Rome has followed his methods and has carried forward her propaganda by cruelty and slaughter. The servants of Christ do not do this.

Nor were *miracles* to be the power. These were useful as establishing the Divine origin of the new thing that God had brought into being, and as guaranteeing the message to be of God. But they were not to be the power by which belief of the Gospel through the coming years was to be secured.

Music was not to be the power, nor *eloquence*, nor *subtle argument*, nor *personal magnetism*, nor *mass psychology*. The Holy Spirit was to be the power, and the heralds of the Gospel were to go forth with the assurance that He would be with them, enabling and empowering them, and backing up their message with the working of His might.

The power of the Holy Spirit was to be for the one purpose of making the witness which was to be borne to Christ effectual. It was not promised that He would empower every preacher, or impart efficacy to every mission. There are those who perhaps with an object quite laudable, would fain *use the Holy Spirit* and thus draw upon His resources of power for the aims that they have in view. But He does not lend Himself to this kind of thing.

On the other hand, if only we will give Him the right of way in connection with our personal lives and service, very graciously *He will use us* to bear effectual witness for Christ.

> " By the Holy Ghost anointed,
>   May we do the Father's will,
> Walk the path by Him appointed,
>   All His pleasure to fulfil."
>
> Thrupp.

THE FOUR COMMUNITIES.

In connection with the Coming of the Holy Spirit there were four communities to be taken into account —(1) Jewish Christians, (2) Samaritan Christians, (3) Gentile Christians, (4) Disciples of John the Baptist. Representatives of all these four companies were baptised with the Holy Spirit, and were thus incorporated into that one Body, where there is neither Jew nor Gentile, but all alike bear the name of Christ.

The baptism with the Spirit of Jewish believers was at Pentecost ; that of Samaritan believers is recorded in Acts viii. 14-17 ; that of Gentile believers in Acts x. 44-46 ; that of John's disciples in Acts xix. 6.

This baptism with the Spirit was never repeated. It was the initiation into Christianity with all its blessings of those who in these four communities had believed in Christ. Those who subsequently believed were not thus baptised with the Spirit, but the Holy Spirit was given to each one at his conversion, to indwell him. Thus those who believed were brought into the one Body. The initial act of baptism with the Spirit was not repeated. The Church was formed, once for all, out of these four communities by the initial act, in the case of each, of baptism with the Spirit. To speak of individuals being baptised with, in, of or by the Holy Spirit to-day is to exhibit singular unintelligence as to its significance.

In the case of communities 1, 3 and 4 baptism with the Spirit was accompanied by the miraculous gift of speaking with " tongues." This, as we learn from Acts ii, was speaking in foreign languages. (The word " other " in verse 4 has the force of " foreign," and is so rendered by some translators.) This is clearly to be distinguished from the speaking with tongues in I Corinthians xii. 30 ; xiii. 8 and xiv. 2-28, 39. We do not read of any speaking with *other* (i.e., foreign) tongues except as a manifestation attending the baptism with the Spirit of the original representatives of three of the above-mentioned communities. It is, therefore, not to be expected to-day.

The gift of speaking in a tongue (in I Corinthians) was an entirely different thing. Those who heard it did not, like those in Acts ii. 11, hear in their own language. They could not understand what was said unless it was interpreted. It seems to have had no place in more spiritual churches, but at Corinth, where they were carnal (I Corinthians iii. 3), it was much to the fore The Apostle urged the Corinthian Christians to lay stress rather on gifts that tended to profit (I Corinthians xiv. 1, 5, 6, 14-19, 22).

The modern pretence of " speaking with tongues " exposes its own falsity by the quality of the " interpretations " given. Many of these are frothy and futile in the extreme. I cannot find one recorded that conveys any spiritual instruction, or anything helpful to souls. If the *real* thing was not to much profit, how very unprofitable must the spurious be!

SEVEN PRINCIPAL WORDS.

Great prominence is given in certain circles to teaching concerning the Baptism of the Holy Spirit. As a result, three classes of persons have arisen :—

1. Persons who profess to have received this " baptism." and who claim to have reached a plane of spiritual experience in advance of that on which the majority of their fellow-Christians dwell.

2. Persons who are bitterly disappointed at the failure of their quest for this " baptism," whose souls, filled with doubt and darkness as a result, become tinged with a measure of unbelief. They often settle down under a cloud of spiritual depression.

3. Persons who declare that they have fulfilled all the conditions but without success. They laughingly say that " there's nothing in it," and call themselves fools for having been " taken in." These are usually very superficial persons, and it is often difficult to distinguish them, in their manner of living, from mere worldlings.

The subject is more or less a controversial one. We shall do well, therefore, to adhere closely to the Scriptures in our consideration of it.

There are SEVEN PRINCIPAL WORDS used in the New

Testament in connection with the presence and work of the Holy Spirit :—

1. Born (John iii. 5, 6).
2. Indwelt (II Timothy i. 14 ; Romans viii. 11).
3. Sealed (II Corinthians i. 22 ; Ephesians i. 13 ; iv. 30).
4. Earnest (II Corinthians i, 22 ; Eph. i. 14).
5. Anointed (II Corinthians i. 21 ; I John ii. 27).
6. Filled (Luke i. 15, 41, 67 ; Acts iv. 8 ; ix. 17, etc.; Ephesians v. 18).
7. Baptized (Matthew iii. 11 ; Acts i. 5 ; I Corinthians xii. 13).

These words are by no means interchangeable ; no two of them mean quite the same. Each has its own significance. This should at once be recognized by all who believe that the very *words* of Scripture are what they are affirmed to be in Psalm xii. 6 : " pure words, as silver tried in a furnace of earth, purified seven times," that is, entirely free from any admixture of human dross. There is a design in the selection and use of the very words of the Scriptures.

Our appeal must always be finally to the Word of God, and not to the experience of ourselves or of others.

THE BAPTISM OF THE SPIRIT : PREDICTIONS.

I am going to ask the reader to join me in a very careful examination of the passages that speak of the Baptism of the Spirit. There are, first, what we may call the prophetic or anticipatory passages, in which predictions are made as to the event which was yet future.

The first is in Matthew iii. 11, where we find John the Baptist saying: "I indeed baptize you with water unto repentance; but He that cometh after me is mightier than I, whose shoes I am not worthy to bear; He shall baptize you with the Holy Ghost and with fire."

There are parallel passages in Mark i. 8 and Luke iii. 16. In John i. 33 is another verse in which the Lord Jesus is indicated as the One who should baptize with the Holy Spirit.

The remaining passage of those that we have called prophetic, or anticipatory, is in Acts i. 5. Here the Lord Himself, after His resurrection, speaks of the promise as yet to be fulfilled, and specifies the time of the Baptism as "not many days" from the time when He was speaking.

These passages from the Gospels and the Acts cover a period of some three years and a half. During the whole of this time the promise remained unfulfilled. The Baptism was still future. Yet during this period the servants of Christ achieved some very remarkable results. They preached the Gospel and healed the sick everywhere they went (Luke ix. 6). They cast out demons (Mark vi. 13) and found them forced to subjection (Luke x. 17). All this, observe, was without any baptism of the Spirit. On one occasion they failed. On their enquiring as to the reason, the Lord did not bid them seek a "baptism of the Spirit," but informed them that the particular kind of demon that they had failed to cast out could only be dealt with by prayer and fasting.

The baptism of the Spirit, therefore, was not necessary for the accomplishment of these wonders, nor for the effectual preaching of the Gospel, while the Lord was on earth. It came to pass at a definite time, after He had gone back to heaven. If we keep this in mind, we shall not be carried away with phrases of Scripture torn from their contexts, nor by doctrines that are based upon a misunderstanding of what the Baptism of the Spirit really was.

BAPTIZED WITH FIRE.

The first passage that speaks of the Baptism of the Spirit (Matthew iii) should be examined with care. The prediction affirms that a time was coming when the Lord Jesus would baptize (1) with the Holy Ghost ; (2) with fire.

With one or the other all who heard John speak would be baptized.

What does the " fire " signify ? It is mentioned in Matthew iii. three times :—

1. Every unfruitful tree would be cast into the *fire* : verse 10.

2. Christ would baptize with *fire* : verse 11.

3. He would burn up those who were mere " chaff " with unquenchable *fire* : verse 12.

Can we resist the conclusion that in these verses the fire signifies *judgment* ? Can it mean one thing in verses 10 and 12, and something entirely different in verse 11 ?

It may be asked : Why should John speak so much of judgment ? The answer lies in the fact that so many were listening to him whom he could only call a " generation of vipers " (verse 7). For them, unless they repented, there was only the baptism of fire, a baptism of " judgment and fiery indignation, which shall devour the adversaries " (Hebrews x. 27).

In Luke iii we find the same thing ; but in Mark i. no mention is made of the baptism with fire, but only of the baptism with the Holy Spirit ; for in that chapter no " generation of vipers " is in view, but a company " confessing their sins " (verse 5).

But all this was to be in the future. The baptizing with the Spirit came within four years. The prediction as to the baptism with fire may have been partially fulfilled during the unspeakably terrible time when Jerusalem was destroyed by the Romans and the temple burnt by their soldiery. But its final fulfilment will, no doubt, take place when " the Lord Jesus shall be revealed from heaven . . . in flaming fire taking vengeance on them that know not God, and that obey not the Gospel of our Lord Jesus Christ " (II Thess. ii. 7, 8).

It is clear, then, that during the life of Christ on earth there was no baptism either with the Spirit or with fire. Every mention of these things related to a time that was then future. That time came when the Holy Spirit descended on the day of Pentecost.

BAPTIZED INTO ONE BODY.

There is one passage which deals with the subject of the Baptism by (or in) the Spirit in what we may call a doctrinal way : I Corinthians xii. 13. " For by one Spirit are we all baptized into one body, whether we be Jews or Gentiles, whether we be bond or free, and have been all made to drink into one Spirit."

The reading in the Revised Version "*were* we all baptized" is preferable to that of the Authorised Version, in that the baptism of the Spirit is not a state or condition, but a definite historic event that had taken place.

Let three things be particularly noticed in this verse.

1. *How many* of the Corinthian believers had been baptized with the Spirit ? ALL. This is distinctly affirmed.

Some of these believers were quarrelsome and sectarian in spirit (i. 11, 12) ; they were carnal, and walked "as men" (iii. 3) ; some were going to law with their brethren before unbelievers (vi. 6); some were even turning the Lord's Supper into an orgy of eating and drinking (xi. 21, 22). They were far from being exemplary Christians. Again and again the apostle rebukes them for their fleshly ways. Yet, since they had truly believed in Christ (Acts xviii. 8) they were children of God, washed, sanctified and justified (vi. 11). As such, they had shared in the baptism of the Spirit ; yes, *all* of them.

2. *With what object* were the Corinthian believers baptized with the Spirit ? Not specially to empower them for testimony and service. At least, this was not the primary object. Nor was it that they might speak with tongues or enjoy any exalted experience. It was that they might be united in one body, one living organism. The great object of the baptism of the Spirit was the formation of the Body of Christ. Believers thereby ceased to be a mere group of individuals brought together by a bond of common interests. By being baptized with the Spirit they were welded into one.

The human body is used as a figure of the Body of Christ, whether in a local sense as in I Corinthians xii, or in its wider sense. Now the human body is not an organization, it is an *organism*, with the same life in every part of it, and governed by the head. We have spoken of this on pages 39 and 40.

No *individual* is ever said to have been baptized with the Spirit. And no individual is ever bidden to seek it. It is a corporate and collective thing. This cannot be too strongly emphasized.

WHEN WERE THEY BAPTIZED ?

On page 49 we remarked that three things were to be specially noticed in reading the thirteenth verse of I Corinthians xii. Now we deal with the third of these.

3. When were the Corinthian believers baptized with the Spirit ? *At no time within their own spiritual experience* !

Let me ask the reader's most careful attention to this point. Unless it be understood, he will never seize the real significance of the Baptism of the Holy Spirit.

By way of illustration read I Corinthians x. 1, 2 : " *All* our fathers were under the cloud, and *all* passed through the sea, and were *all* baptized unto Moses." Well, we read of some of the " fathers " in Acts xxviii. 25. They lived some hundreds of years after the crossing of the Red Sea, yet it is said : " *All* our fathers were under the cloud, and *all* passed through the sea."

Again, Jehovah says to His erring people in Amos ii. 10 : " I brought YOU up from the land of Egypt, and led YOU forty years through the wilderness." As a matter of fact the people thus addressed had never been in Egypt or the wilderness. They lived hundreds of years after the Exodus. Yet they are said to have shared in that wonderful deliverance.

In like manner, the Corinthian believers had not been actually present on the occasion of the great historic Baptism of the Spirit. But just as the " fathers " of Isaiah's day, and the Israelites addressed by **Amos were** spoken of as having been the subjects of the great deliverance from Egypt, in that by their birth as Israelites they had become a part of the people thus favoured by God, so the Christians at Corinth are spoken of as having been baptized by the Spirit in that they, being indwelt by the Spirit of God through their reception of the Gospel, had become a part of the wonderful organism, the Body of Christ.

Personally and literally neither the Corinthian Christians (nor any who have lived subsequently) were baptized with the Spirit, any more than those referred to in Amos ii. 10 were personally and literally brought up from Egypt. But each one, as he received the Gospel, was sealed with the Spirit of God, thus becoming an integral part of that company which was formed by the Baptism of the Spirit into one body.

THE ACTUAL EVENT.

We now come to the third group of passages that relate to the Baptism of the Spirit—the historical, or narrative, Scriptures that describe, or refer to, the actual event.

Acts ii. is the chapter that gives us in detail the account of how the Lord's promise that the disciples should " be baptized with the Holy Ghost not many days hence " (Acts i. 5) was fulfilled. The actual words " baptism " and " baptize " are not used in this chapter with reference to this great event, but that it *was* the promised baptism is abundantly clear from Acts i. 5 ; xi. 15, 16.

It is spoken of as a *pouring forth* of the Spirit (Acts ii. 33, R.V.). And a later *pouring out* of the Spirit (Acts x. 45, to which we shall presently refer) is said to have been made after the same manner as the way He was given at Pentecost: " as on us at the beginning " (Acts xi. 15).

Again, we notice, as in I Cor. xii., the word *all*. The hundred and twenty disciples, mean and women, were *all* with one accord in one place. Suddenly the Spirit was " poured forth " and filled them *all* (verse 4). The baptism included every one present, and the result was, that the Body of Christ was formed. The hundred and twenty became members of a living organism, united to their Head in heaven in this wonderful way.

There were other results. A sound was heard as of a rushing mighty wind ; cloven tongues, like as of a fire, sat on each disciple. Previously God had made His angels winds (Heb. i. 7, R.V.) and a flame of fire. If God desired to make some great wind blow in the souls of men, or some fire of zeal and enthusiasm to burn and glow, He brought it to pass by the service of His angels. But that was superseded at Pentecost by the gift of the Spirit. Henceforward *He* would be the origin of any mighty wind of God among the sons of men ; *He* would be the author of any bright flame that God should kindle.

Now, in that the disciples were all " filled with the Holy Ghost " when the Baptism took place, people have confounded the historic Baptism with the *filling* which continuously takes place, and which is enjoined upon all Christians (Ephesians v. 18). We are exhorted to be *filled*, but, as before remarked, never to be *baptized* with the Spirit. The difference is real and important. But of this more anon.

THE SIGN GIFTS.

The earnest desire for this " filling " (or " baptism " with the Spirit as it is wrongly called) on the part of many is that they may receive power for effective service, or that they may be enabled to speak with " tongues " and perform other remarkable exploits. But such control, even by the Spirit of God Himself, does not imply a state of real communion with God, or of real love to Him.

Balaam was a man thus controlled by the Spirit of God (Numbers xxiv. 2). He was forced to utter true and wonderful things. But he himself was an evil man, a lover of gain (Jude 11) and a corrupter of others (Rev. ii. 14). Saul, afterwards King of Israel, was a man thus possessed on one occasion by the Spirit of God (1 Samuel x. 6 and 10). He was " turned into another man " (that is, he was changed from a clumsy, country youth into a kingly man who could fill the throne with dignity) and made to open his mouth in prophecy. It was a wonderful " sign " (verse 7) every bit as wonderful as anything done by the claimants to a special endowment of the Spirit to-day ; yet Saul remained an unregenerate man, going further and further from God, and dying under the sentence of His anger. The possession of " sign gifts," then, is no proof of holiness or real devotion.

Yet the "signs" that accompanied the historic gift of the Spirit, and which seem to have lingered in the churches during at least the first part of the life of the apostles, were of real importance in that they marked the ushering in of a new era. It had been so before when God called Israel to be His people, their birth as a nation and their deliverance from Gentile tyranny were marked by mighty "signs" and miracles in Egypt (Psalm cv. 27).

It will be so again in the future. When the present period is ended, and the millennial age begins, its beginning will be marked by a great outpouring of the Spirit, accompanied by "wonders" (Joel ii. 28-31).

Through the Acts of the Apostles, particularly in chapters i to xii, the narrative deals with an initiatory and transitional state of things. To this period "speaking with tongues" and similar "signs" were confined. Throughout the history of Paul's life and work, we search in vain for any hint of a Baptism with the Spirit which some believers may be without, which is evidenced by speaking with tongues, and which has to be sought.

THE ABIDING PRESENCE OF THE HOLY SPIRIT.

Our Lord's promise that the other Comforter that was to come would abide with His disciples for ever, or, if the translation be preferred, "for the age" (John xiv. 16) was to be taken literally. And all that His coming at Pentecost inaugurated continues to this day. We are still in the period of the Holy Spirit's residence on earth.

Is not this fact overlooked to a large extent, even in evangelical circles? What else but the ignoring of His presence are these repeated requests to Him to come ? these hymns that voice appeals to Him to descend ?

A nobleman kindly promises to take the chair at a public meeting, and duly arrives at the appointed hour. But the conveners do not recognize him, and begin to be anxious. They telephone to his residence, begging him to come, only to be informed that his lordship started for the meeting half an hour previously. They send a messenger, hoping that he will meet with the expected chairman on the way, and expedite his arrival. All this while his lordship stands there waiting to be recognized, ready to take the chair and open the proceedings as he had promised. He speaks to one or two, but they seem too busy to attend to what he says. He addresses one of the conveners, but the good man rushes off without listening to a word. His presence is ignored, while messages beseeching him to come are despatched.

Is not the situation similar with regard to the Holy Spirit ? He came, as was promised, at Pentecost. He is still here, ready to fill His place, and take charge on behalf of Christ.

Instead of praying " Descend, O Holy Ghost, descend," or " Come, Heavenly Dove," why not recognize Him as present, cease to usurp His functions of leadership, and give Him the right of way ? Those who do this are never the losers. Their personal lives and their corporate lives are vastly the richer for their acknowledgment of the presence and leadership of the Holy Spirit.

> *" Jesus, the Bread of life, is given*
> *To be our daily food ;*
> *Within us dwells that spring from heaven,*
> *The Spirit of our God."*
>
> J. Newton.

THE COMFORTER.

Four times in the Gospel of John Christ spoke of the Holy Spirit, who was to come to His disciples after His departure, as the Comforter.

In the first instance the Lord referred to Him as *another* Comforter (John xiv. 16). He had Himself been the Comforter and Preserver of His loved ones. Now it was necessary for Him to leave them. But Another would come Who would be to them what He had been, and who would never depart, but remain with them for ever.

Secondly, the promised Comforter would teach them all things (John xv. 26). There was so much that the disciples failed to understand of what the Lord had said to them. Moreover, there was so much that He did not say to them, because of their dullness of understanding (xvi. 12). But the Holy Spirit would make everything clear and instruct them in all that was necessary. And He would recall for them the sayings of Christ.

Thirdly, the Comforter would be the Spirit of truth, and would testify of Christ (John xv. 26). Of this we have spoken in another place.

Lastly, He would take a certain attitude with regard to the world (John xvi. 7-11); reproving (or convicting) the world with reference to sin, righteousness and judgment.

The English word "Comforter" does not give the full meaning of the word which the Saviour used, which (in its English form) was Paraclete. It is the same word that is rendered "Advocate" in 1 John ii. 1. It means one who looks after the interests of others, especially of those who are his dependents.

There is an abstract noun, *paraklesis*, of the same derivation, which is used in Acts ix. 31 : " the comfort of the Holy Ghost." It has also the force of encouragement and help. We may with equal correctness translate the word " Comforter " by " Helper," and think of the Holy Spirit as our truest and best Helper on earth.

As to the real force of His title " the Spirit of truth " we speak on pages 58 and 59.

THE HELPER.

In his " New Translation," Dr. Moffatt renders the word Comforter by " Helper," in all the four passages in the Gospel of John where it occurs.

The late Dr. Torrey gives an encouraging example of what it means to have the Holy Spirit with us as our Divine Helper. He says :

" I entered the minstry because I was obliged to. My conversion turned upon my preaching. For years I refused to be a Christian because I was determined that I would not preach. The night I was converted I did not say ' I will accept Christ,' or anything of that sort. I said ' I will preach.'

" But if any man was never fitted by natural temperament to preach, it was I. I was abnormally timid. I never even spoke in a prayer meeting until after I had entered the theological seminary. My first attempt to do so was an agonizing experience. In my early ministry I wrote my sermons out and committed them to memory, and when the evening service came to a close and I had uttered the last word of the sermon, I would sink back with a sense of great relief that that was over for another week. Preaching was torture.

" But the glad day came when I got hold of the thought, and the thought got hold of me, that when I stood up to preach Another stood by my side, and though the audience saw me, the responsibility was really upon Him, and that He was perfectly competent to bear it, and all I had to do was to stand back and get as far out of sight as possible, and let Him do the work which the Father sent Him to do.

" From that day preaching has not been a burden, nor a duty, but a glad privilege. I have no anxiety nor care. I know that He is conducting the service and doing it just as it ought to be done. And even though things may not seem to go just as I think they ought, I know they have gone right. Oftentimes when I get up to preach, and the thought takes possession of me that He is there to do it all, such a joy fills my heart that I feel like shouting for very ecstasy."

But it is not only preachers and other Christian workers who need, and who have, the Holy Spirit as their ready Helper. He will be our Helper, if only we make room for Him, in all the things that we have to face in the round of everyday duty. He will be our Helper in the shop, the office, the schoolroom or the home. And His help is wonderful !

THE SPIRIT OF TRUTH.

Connected with this title of the Holy Spirit our Lord made a prediction of the utmost importance : " When He, the Spirit of truth, is come, *He will guide you into all truth* " (John xvi. 13). We must emphasize the " you " in this promise. Christ was speaking to His apostles, and the promise was made exclusively to them.

It was repeated in another form in John xiv. 26 : " He shall teach you all things."

That the promise was not intended to apply to all Christians is surely evident. Who, save the apostles, can say " I have been guided into ALL truth," or " The Holy Spirit has taught me ALL things ? "

The meaning of the promise appears to be this. While partial revelations of the truth were made to the old-time prophets, and further unfoldings given by Christ when on earth, finality would be reached when the Holy Spirit came. He would utter, through the apostles, the final word. No subsequent revelation was to be expected. The truth was to be delivered once for all to the saints (Jude 3). The Holy Spirit would guide the apostles into *all* truth.

It is the personal guarantee of Christ that the final revelation of God : His counsels, His love, His ways, which we find in the writings of the apostles, proceeds from the Holy Spirit.

A further guarantee is given in the latter part of John xiv. 26 : " He shall . . . bring all things to your remembrance, whatsoever I have said unto you." The Gospels, therefore, are not the product of the unaided memories of their writers. They are the record of what the Holy Spirit brought to their remembrance. And He brought to their remembrance ALL the things which Jesus had spoken, and which it was the will of God that they should relate.

Yet another promise was made at the end of John xiv. 13 : " He will shew you things to come." Here we have our Lord's guarantee of the prophetic book of the New Testament, the Revelation. This book was not written that people who witnessed the fulfilment of the prophecies should be helped and guided thereby, but that the Lord might " shew unto His servants things which must shortly come to pass " (Rev. i. 1). This is in full accord with the promise of John xvi. 13.

So the Spirit of truth is the *real* Author of the New Testament. The teachings of the apostles are *His* teachings. This is guaranteed by the three-fold promise of the Lord. And the New Testament has given us God's *final word* to us while we are on earth.

RESISTING THE HOLY SPIRIT.

There are various ways in which the Holy Spirit is opposed, and His work hindered.

1. Resisting Him (Acts vii. 51).
2. Grieving Him (Ephesians iv. 30).
3. Quenching Him (I Thessalonians v. 19).

We will first consider what Resisting Him means.

The Spirit of God had been striving mightily with the men of Israel, seeking to lead them to repentance and to acceptance of Christ. Many times they had refused to hearken. Once more, through the mouth of Stephen, He addresses them in Acts vii., but the only result was that " they were cut to the heart, and gnashed on him with their teeth." How true is the awful charge brought against them in verse 51 : " Ye do always resist the Holy Ghost."

What the Holy Spirit was then doing in the case of the nation of Israel He is doing to-day with individuals. He strives with men, seeking to lead them to the Saviour's feet in true repentance and faith. But alas ! many, follow in the steps of those to whom Stephen spoke. They hear the gospel, the need of their deathless souls is presented to them and in measure they are impressed. But other things come in and divert their attention. Their impressions wear off. The uneasy feeling dies away, and they resume the old routine of life as careless as ever. *They have resisted the Holy Ghost* !

Is their doom for ever sealed, then ? By no means. Though often resisted, the Spirit of God is full of grace. Indeed, He is called " the Spirit of grace." In mercy He may strive again. Once more the soul may be brought to serious consideration. Is He still resisted, and His voice silenced ? Then in patient grace He may strive yet again.

But lest His patience should be used by men as an excuse for trifling with Him, one solemn fact is recorded in the Bible by God Himself. " My Spirit *shall not always* strive with man " (Gen. vi. 3).

No one can say how often, or for how long, the Holy Ghost will strive with a man, but when He ceases nothing will ever reach that man's soul. He may listen to the story of God's love, he may have the gospel plainly set before him, but there will be no response, no real conviction of sin or desire for salvation.

If any man has a desire for salvation, it shows that the Holy Spirit is still striving with him, and his only wise and safe course is to come at once to Christ for pardon. He will assuredly receive it, and be blessed.

The sin of resisting the Holy Spirit must not be confounded with that of " *blasphemy* against the Holy Ghost." For *that* sin there is no forgiveness (Mark iii. 28). With this we shall deal at length in a future chapter.

GRIEVING THE HOLY SPIRIT.

Let the passage which mentions this sin (Ephesians iv. 30) be read carefully. It is frequently quoted as if the words were: " Grieve not *away* the Holy Spirit." But the word " away " is not there. Indeed, there is no such thing as a Christian grieving away the Holy Spirit. The very verse that warns against grieving Him states that we " are sealed unto the day of redemtpion." Of this we have spoken on pages 36 and 37.

The Christian belongs to Christ. Bought by His precious blood, he is His " purchased possession." By-and-by the Saviour is coming to claim us. Our suffering bodies will be released from all that makes us groan ; aches and pains, trials and temptations, sin and sorrow, will all be things of the past. That will be redemption in its fulness. And it is until that day that we " were sealed with that Holy Spirit of promise." It does not say " until He is grieved away," but " until the redemption of the purchased possession."

Does not this passage very clearly teach that the Christian is sealed with the Holy Ghost for as long as he is on earth ? Does it not confirm the promise of the Lord Himself that the Comforter should abide with us *for ever* ? (John xiv. 16). Christ is coming soon to take possession of " His own," and meanwhile the Holy Ghost is in charge of us, and will not leave us.

Suppose that a gentleman intends to spend a year or so in foreign travel. Instead of shutting up his house and storing his furniture, he engages a caretaker to take charge of it during his absence. For a time all goes well, but one day a loud crash is heard in one of the rooms. The caretaker rushes upstairs and finds that a large piece of plaster has fallen from the drawing-room ceiling, breaking some of the furniture, and covering the rest with dust.

Naturally he is grieved, but he does not on that account pack up his trunk and take his departure. Leaving his ordinary duties, he devotes his attention to repairing the damage. He calls in the plasterer to put the ceiling in good order. The broken furniture is place in the hands of the upholsterer, and the whole room is cleared of the dirt and dust.

This illustrates what takes place when a believer grieves the Holy Spirit. Too faithful a Caretaker to depart, He devotes His attention to repairing the spiritual damage in our souls. He desists from His normal occupation of ministering joy and comfort to our hearts, and seeks to lead us to self-judgment and confession, in order that we may be restored.

WHAT GRIEVES HIM ?

It is sometimes asked : " What is it to grieve the Holy Spirit ? Is it by lying, stealing, swearing, or doing any other wicked thing ?

This is an important question. Needless to say, if a Christian should sin like this it would greatly grieve the Holy Spirit. He is the HOLY Spirit and is necessarily grieved by anything unholy. But He may be much grieved even by one whose outward conduct is quite exemplary.

Suppose that while visiting at a friend's house my kind hostess shows me an album with photos in it. Pointing to one, she says: " This is a very dear relative of mine, who is away in South Africa," and she speaks in glowing terms of his life and doings. All at once looking up, she finds me gazing out of the window, occupied with something going on in the street.

My inattention grieves my kind hostess. " It is of no use my showing him the album," she says to herself, " he is not a bit interested." So she closes the book and lays it aside.

Now the Holy Spirit is here, as it were, with a wonderful album of pictures. The pictures are all of the same glorious Person, and the Holy Spirit is intent upon describing to us His beauty, His love, and His glory.

If, instead of listening to Him, we are gazing in another direction, occupied with the things of the world, or taken up with other objects, He will be grieved, and *will close the album*. That is to say, He will cease ministering Christ to our hearts, and will rebuke us by withholding joy and comfort from our souls.

What, then, is to be done when we have grieved the Holy Spirit ?

I will ask, What should I do when, in the foregoing illustration, I have grieved my hostess by being so inattentive ? At once apologise for my rudeness, and on my expressing regret the lady might once again open the album and continue her conversation. In like manner, when we have grieved the Holy Spirit, our first duty is to confess our folly. We should go to God our Father and ask Him to make us feel the seriousness of it, and pray for grace to be more attentive in the future. If our self-judgment is real, the Holy Spirit will again make us conscious of the Father's love, and will enable us afresh to rejoice in the Lord.

BITTER MEMORIES.

" Why is it that I know so little of this joy in the Lord ? " one may ask. And the question will bring bitter memories with it, for there was a time (was there not ?) when you were no stranger to this joy. Your heart was filled in those bygone days with the love of Christ. How precious He was to you then ! What delight you found in prayer, and in communing with Him over the Word !

But now all is changed. Where once sweet flowers grew there seems now to be nothing but noisome weeds. Discordant sounds have taken the place of heavenly melody. The joy, the sweetness, the communion which you once experienced are now nothing but a recollection.

> " These happy hours I once enjoyed,
>   How sweet their memory still !
> But they have left an aching void
>   That nothing seems to fill."

The story is told of a lady who sat down before a grand organ and ran her fingers over its keys. While thus employed, she struck a chord of music which thrilled her whole being with its majestic melody. But when she tried to strike that chord again, she could not. Long she tried, but in vain. It was *a lost chord.*

Does anyone read these lines out of whose life the music had died away ? You remember that chord of joy which one vibrated within you. Where is it now ? " Where is then the blessedness ye spake of ?" It has vanished ; the melody has ceased ; that chord of heavenly joy is a lost chord.

The question of questions for you, then, is : " Can I recover it ? And how ? What must I do that once again my life may be flooded with brightness and my heart filled with joy?"

Read the fourteenth chapter of Hosea. Verse 1 tells us that God really wants to restore His backsliding children. We may be sure, therefore, that He will place no difficulty in their way. He directs them to *take with them words*, as they turn to the Lord. First, words of prayer and confession. Second, words of promise, "So will we render." Third, words of renunciation, "Asshur shall not save us." Fourth, words of confidence, "In Thee the fatherless findeth mercy." These verses indicate the exercises of soul that befit the one who seeks restoration to communion with God. They are followed by His own gracious promise: "I will heal their backsliding; I will love them freely."

SELF-OCCUPATION.

One of the greatest hindrances to our regaining the happiness which we forfeited by our coldness and backsliding is our occupation with ourselves. By some form of religious self-culture we try to improve that which cannot be improved. Even to make happiness, victory over sin, or service, our object is a subtle form of this terrible thing: self-occupation.

It is good to "call to remembrance the former days," to examine one's ways and to judge one's self unsparingly. But this of itself can never bring back the joy.

The writer was once shown into a room where a little girl sat playing a simple air upon the piano. Evidently confused by the presence of a visitor, she commenced to strike many wrong notes. Then, taking her eyes from the music before her, she began to look at her fingers, and endeavoured to place them on the right notes. Needless to say, the mistakes became worse than before, and presently she broke down altogether and stopped playing.

Looking at her own fingers was the worst thing the girl could have done. If she had kept her eye fixed on the sheet of music in front of her, she might have corrected her mistakes and continued playing.

So if we get occupied with ourselves and our failures, our coldness and our lack of power, we shall surely break down. That is not the way of recovery. But while truly judging ourselves for our carelessness and folly, if we look away to Christ, and seek His presence, it may be—nay, it *will* be—that the chord that was lost will again be struck !

In this we shall have the gracious and potent help of the Holy Spirit. For in looking away from self to Christ, and having Him before our minds, we are doing the very opposite to grieving the Holy Spirit. We are *pleasing* Him.

A little thing may grieve Him ; a little indifference to what He wants to lead us to enjoy ; a little inattention to His minstrelsy of love. On the other hand, a little thing will please Him. A little desire to know more of Christ ; a little longing to be better instructed in the purposes of God ; this will greatly please the Holy Spirit, and will secure His loving and ready help.

THE LOST CHORD REGAINED.

If the lady seated before the organ, trying in vain to place her fingers on the notes that she had struck, could have had a wise and gracious helper, she might have found the lost chord again. Suppose that a skilful, guiding hand had been placed over hers, moving her fingers to the right keys, what a difference it would have made!

There is One who can do this for us, and that is the Holy Spirit. The point for us to settle is whether we will permit Him to have His gracious way with us.

A stranger once entered the grand cathedral of Freiburg and asked permission to play on its world-famed organ.

The organist in charge at first refused. But after much persuasion, and perhaps a gratuity, he was prevailed upon to allow him to play, and he sat down before the organ.

His fingers brought from the instrument the most wonderful music. The organist was entranced and spell-bound. At last he turned to the player and said—

" May I ask your name, sir ? "

" Mendelssohn ! " replied the visitor, who was indeed no other than the great composer himself.

" And to think that I refused *you* persmission ! " the man answered.

Just as Mendelssohn wished to play the Freiburg organ, the Holy Ghost desires to produce music in our hearts and lives. Alas ! how often He is met by a refusal ! How often we hinder Him ! How many of us, when we look back upon our lives, will have to exclaim self-reproachfully in the words of the organist—

" To think that I refused YOU permission ! "

Let us arise from our sleep ! Let us seek grace to put away all hindrances to the Holy Spirit's having entire control of us. Let us cease to grieve Him by being inattentive to His ministry, and indifferent to the One whom He desires to make *everything* to our hearts.

Then He will be able to fill us once again with joy. It will be ours once more to drink the sweet waters of communion, and the power which we have lacked will again make itself felt in our lives and testimony. Prayer will be an enjoyed and valued privilege. We shall delight to study the Scriptures, and our eyes will be opened to see wonderful things in the sacred pages.

QUENCHING THE SPIRIT.

It must be remembered that one of the great purposes for which the Holy Spirit has taken up His residence on earth is the formation of the Church, the Body and Bride of Christ.

He also works to gather those who believe into churches, which, in the locality where they are found, shall be lampstands upon which Christ may set His light.

In the early days of Christianity *all* the Christians in a given locality were wont to assemble in one place. We read of this again and again.

At Jerusalem " they were all with one accord *in one place* " (Acts ii. 1). At Troas, " the disciples *came together* to break bread " (Acts xx. 7). At Corinth the custom was for " the whole church " to " come together into one place " (I Corinthians xiv. 23).

These passages show us how the Christians in New Testament times acknowledged their unity by coming together for prayer, for the breaking of bread, or for edification. And a careful reading of I Corinthians xiv. will show that the way was left open for the Holy Spirit to use whom He would, and as many as He would, to take part in the meeting.

In later days there arose a tendency to centralize the various gifts of the Holy Spirit in one man. Some, whose language perhaps was not as cultured as it might have been, were refused a hearing. Against this tendency Paul utters a needed word of warning. " Quench not the Spirit ; despise not prophesyings," he says (I Thess. v. 19, 20).

The tendency referred to inevitably results in a quenching of the Spirit. If human arrangement be allowed to take the place of divine order ; if men be appointed to officiate instead of guidance being left to the Holy Spirit, it practically quenches Him in the gatherings of the saints.

I am not now speaking of meetings which are held by evangelists, or by teachers for the exercise of their ministry. Nor do I refer to Conferences, where all, Christians and unconverted people, sit together. Such are not, in principle, assemblies of the saints. I am referring to meetings for worship, for the breaking of bread, or for prayer. If all the gifts and ministrations are centralized in one man, to the exclusion of others whom the Spirit might be pleased to use, in such a meeting the Holy Spirit is practically quenched.

What was only a tendency in the days of the apostles has become an established custom in ours. But the custom is none the less evil because it is established. If it is a sad thing for an unregenerate man to *resist* the Holy Spirit, and for a believer to *grieve* Him, it is equally sad when a religious community systematically *quenches* Him.

LYING TO THE HOLY SPIRIT.

This sin is not to be confounded with any of those of which we have spoken, though it must assuredly have greatly grieved the Holy Spirit. Others have lied in the same way that Ananias and his wife did, lied about money, lied about property, lied for the sake of gain. Yet others have lied far more foully and persistently. Wherein, then, lay the peculiar awfulness of the sin that made Peter say to the guilty individual : " Why hath Satan filled thine heart to lie to the Holy Ghost ? " (Acts v. 3).

It was a time of tremendous spiritual power. Everything was regarded as secondary to the claims of the new faith. Those who were " all filled with the Holy Ghost " (Acts iv. 31), and indeed all the believers, were parting with their property, making what would be called in days when enthusiasm had cooled " great sacrifices." The Holy Spirit had inaugurated a wonderful movement, and multitudes were mightily stirred in their new-born faith and devotion to Christ.

To introduce a contrary element into such an atmosphere as this that had been created was a most serious thing. To have anything to do with the movement was to have to do with the Spirit of God, for the movement was His. To bring in falsity and deceit was a sin of no ordinary magnitude ; it was to lie to the Holy Spirit.

Ananias and Sapphira evidently thought that their lie would go undetected. They were going to put the matter to the test, for, as Peter says, they had " agreed together to tempt the Spirit of the Lord." When thus tested, He was found to be omniscient, all-discerning, holy and powerful. The sin met with instant doom.

In later times of spiritual revival it has been observed that sin takes on an added seriousness, and sin in connection with the revival, or in one who takes a prominent part in it, had not infrequently been met as the sin of Ananias and Sapphira, by the transgressor being cut off.

Those who so ardently desire "another Pentecost" should bear this in mind. For Pentecost meant, among other things, that sin was at once discerned and met with immediate retribution.

The presence of the Holy Spirit has its solemn, as well as its blessed side. To bring sin into the place where He dwells, the assembly, is to corrupt "the temple of God" (I Corinthians iii. 17). Let us lay the warning to heart.

THE EARNEST.

Speaking of the glorious and certain future that awaits us, Paul tells us that God Himself has "wrought us" for it, and has also given us the earnest of the Spirit (II Corinthians v. 5). He is thus the Earnest of the inheritance that awaits us (Ephesians i. 14).

As the Seal He is given us on God's behalf, to secure for God what is His, and what is to be for His glory for ever. But as the Earnest He is given to us for *our* comfort and assurance, in our hearts (II Corinthians i. 22).

But there is more than this in the word translated "earnest." The Holy Spirit, given to us, is the pledge that we shall one day be put in possession of the inheritance reserved in heaven for us. But more, He is the *instalment* of that inheritance, the means by which we may already enter into the reality and joy of it. One learned and competent translator, in his "New Translation," renders the word for earnest "pledge and instalment" both in 2 Corinthians v. 5 and Ephesians i. 14.

It is like this. I am going on a voyage overseas, and I promise to take my boy, a lad of twelve, with me. For his enjoyment on board the ship I buy him a telescope, not a mere toy, but a serviceable instrument. The gift is an assurance to him on my part that I intend to take him on the voyage.

But it is more than that. When the voyage is nearly ended word goes round the ship that land is in sight. I can see nothing, but my boy, with his telescope to his eye, says he can see the hills quite clearly. Soon I can trace the outlines of the hills, but my boy exclaims : "I can see the trees and some houses." These things a little later can be just discerned by unaided sight, but the lad sings out : "Father, I can see the people down on the wharf."

The telescope gives him a clearer vision of the land to which he is going. It enables him to get glimpses of it before he arrives. That is what the Holy Spirit as the Earnest does for us. There is a hymn that says :
"The Spirit grants the sight
Of that resplendent One."

That is it ; He gives us keener spiritual vision ; He brings within the arena of present enjoyment the great things that constitute our eternal inheritance ; He enables us already, as it were, to breathe the atmosphere of heaven, and to gain acquaintance with what is there.

All this would be made good to us increasingly if only we walked in the power of an ungrieved Spirit, and gave Him the right of way in our lives.

THE FIELD OF CLOVER.

May I be permitted a few further words as to the thesis of this chapter ? It is important that we should lay hold of the great truth that the thought of the Earnest is not merely that present assurance as to our glorious future is given us through the indwelling of the Holy Spirit, but a positive foretaste of what awaits us.

I remember hearing, when quite a youth, an address on this subject by the late George Cutting. His well thought out illustrations always threw a flood of light on the matter of which he was treating, and possessed a positively evidential value.

He pictured a farmer buying some sheep at a market, and entrusting them to his man to take them safely home.

" Turn them into the enclosure by the barn, John," he said. " And cut a few armfuls of that sweet clover from the field behind the house, and put them into the enclosure for the sheep to feed on this evening. To-morrow, we will turn them out into the field itself."

Does not this exactly describe the situation ? We are the sheep that have been purchased and entrusted to the care of the Holy Spirit to be conducted home. In the glorious by-and-by for which we wait, we are going to be turned into a wonderful field of clover, so to speak. Meanwhile, the Holy Spirit, as the Earnest of the inheritance, gives us tastes of that sweet clover. He brings armfuls of it for our present enjoyment. Things which will be actually ours when we get to heaven are made real to us now.

Let us, then, do something more than continually thank God that He has given us the Earnest. The Holy Spirit opens to us the garden of God's delights. Let us walk through the length and breadth thereof. By *faith* we know that all is ours ; by *the power of the Spirit* we appropriate and enjoy it : a different thing altogether.

" Borne by His power, our souls in strength
    Would tread that realm above :
Its height and depth, its breadth and length,
    And know Christ's love."
Edward Whyte.

POSSESSED.

It is a sad fact that a great many Christians are satisfied to know that the Holy Spirit indwells them, and will never leave them, without being exercised as to letting Him control and dominate them. Is the reader one of these ? You are able to praise God that *you possess the Holy Ghost* ; but the question you have to face is this : *Does the Holy Ghost possess you ?*

There are different kinds of " possessed " people in the world. In the Gospels we read of those who were possessed by demons. Mary Magdalene was one such. Her poor body was the dwelling place of seven devils. Then there are the *self-possessed* people. Their name is legion. One meets them in every town—quiet proper, respectable Christian people, priding themselves upon their moderation and the impossibility of *their* ever being carried away by an excess of zeal or enthusiasm ! Listen to their public prayers ; how correct their words, how calm their manner, how utterly free from anything approaching that *fervour* which is one of the conditions of a righteous man's prayers being answered (James v. 16). Are they happy ?

Gladly, then, will we leave them to such happiness as they enjoy.

Besides these there are in the world *Holy Ghost possessed* men and women. Would to God that we could say that their name too is legion!

Unworldly in their thought, self-sacrificing in their lives, earnest and devoted in their efforts to bring others to the Saviour, possessing power with God in prayer, everything about them witnesses to the fact that the Holy Ghost has taken possession of them for Christ, filling their eyes with the sight of His glory, their lips with His praise and their hearts with His love. For when the Holy Spirit takes possession of anyone it is *on behalf of Christ*, in order that Christ may be paramount in that person's affections and prominent in his life.

Shall we not pray earnestly that many such Christ-possessed, Holy Spirit-dominated men, may be raised up in these days of coldness and declension? Let us pray that we ourselves may be among the number. And what we pray for, let us go in for whole-heartedly.

FILLED WITH THE SPIRIT.

That to be " filled with the Spirit " is a further step than being indwelt or sealed is evident from the fact that the very persons who are assured that they *are* sealed are exhorted to *be* " filled " (Ephesians v. 18).

Nowhere within the covers of the Bible do we find an exhortation to be *sealed* with the Spirit. In that matter we have no option. But with regard to being *filled* it is far otherwise. It is for us to choose whether or not we shall earnestly and prayerfully seek to know the further blessedness of being " filled with the Spirit."

In treating of this subject we must remember that no vessel can be filled with one thing without being emptied of another. In order to be filled with the Spirit one must be prepared to part with all contrary things that have a place in one's heart and mind. Things which hinder communion will have to be given up if one is to be thus filled.

We should seek to be filled with the Spirit. But let us be clear that God *does not fill us with His Spirit from the outside, but from the inside.*

A visitor to your house does not fill it. He is confined to that part of the house to which you have introduced him. If, however, you put your whole house at his disposal, and give him the key of every room and cupboard, he then *fills* the establishment. It is not that he comes in from outside. He is already there ; but now he is, by your act of surrender, in complete control.

Even so it is with the Holy Spirit. We often confine Him to certain parts of our experience and life. But He desires to be in full control, to possess us entirely on behalf of Christ. When we gladly yield to His control the whole establishment of our being, He is then in undisputed charge, and in this sense fills us. How simple, and how *reasonable*, the truth is !

I remember going, when quite a boy, from sheer curiosity to a meeting advertised as " Three Hours with God." It was a kind of pandemonium, dozens of people praying aloud at the same time. I sat near a man who was on his knees, perspiring and pleading, holding out the top of his waistcoat as if it were a bag, and shouting : " Pour it in, Lord ! Pour it in, Lord ! " His prayer consisted of nothing but the repetition of this. But God does not bestow the Holy Spirit after that fashion !

FILLED AND EMPTIED.

I hope my reader did not regard as a mere axiom the statement that no vessel can be filled with one thing without being emptied of another. It is also true that, except by certain apparatus for producing a vacuum, no vessel can be emptied of one thing unless it be filled with another.

This suggests a question of great practical moment in connection with our being filled with the Holy Spirit. Must we be emptied in order to be filled ? Or are we filled in order to be emptied ?

A prominent school of teachers pronounces the former to be the right method. Earnest people are set to rid themselves of the hindrances by continuous prayer and fasting, by self-mortification and patient, persistent endeavour. But, somehow or other, the plan does not work.

Suppose that I hold in my hand a glass, apparently empty. In reality it is full of air. How may I empty it of this ? Not by frantically shaking it in an upside down position. Not by wiping it out with a cloth. It may be emptied by the simple plan of standing it quietly on the table and filling it with water. I empty it of the one thing by filling it with the other.

There are things in our Christian lives that have no business to be there. There are unworthy motives, impure thoughts, covetous desires, selfishness and all manner of things. They need to be cast out as surely as the sellers of oxen and the changers of money needed to be driven from the Temple. But be it noticed that in John ii. *the filling of the water-pots comes first* ; the emptying of the temple follows.

This is the order. When we look up into the face of Christ, not so much with the eyes of trustful faith, as

THE HOLY SPIRIT Here Today 79

with eyes of affection; when He becomes attractive to our hearts, His Spirit fills us on His behalf, and the evil things are crowded out. We experience what Dr. Chalmers called " the expulsive power of a new affection." The attractiveness of Christ makes the things of the world seem tawdry, and the ways of sin repulsive.

SHUT THE GATE.

In seeking the filling for the sake of Christ, and not merely as the means of clearing our hearts and thoughts of evil things, there is one thing that must never be forgotten.

In order to present this thought forcibly I am going to relate in an accurate manner something that I once saw. Let the reader discern where the error in the story lies.

I stood by a lock on a deep American waterway. To my left the water stood at a high level, maintained thus by the strong lock gate that held it back. Between the two gates the water was down very low and the stream to my right was at the same level as this. The gate to my right having slowly opened an oil-tanker glided into the lock. Then the strong gate to my left was gradually swung back, the level of the water in the lock was rapidly raised to the level of that on my left. The tanker was raised with it, and resumed its journey upstream.

My story, as it stands, is palpably false. Yet I saw all this with my own eyes. But I have omitted a detail. And that detail is vital. It is this. After the tanker had glided into the lock *the gate to my right was firmly closed.* Otherwise the incoming waters would never have raised the level of the water between the gates; they would simply have run away downstream and have been wasted.

Do you see the application of this to the matter of which we have spoken? When you open your heart to the treasures of love which Christ can pour therein, when the Spirit fills you and controls your life on His behalf, do not omit to close that other gate: the gate of your life that leads out into the world of sin. *Keep that gate closed* or the tide of blessing and joy will run away and be lost.

" Thou, when thou prayest, enter into thy closet, and . . . shut the door,"—not only the literal door of the room, but the door of your innermost soul. At the same time, be sure that you have the *open window* as well as the closed door. Be like Daniel. Keep your soul's window open to the great things of God, your soul's door closed to all that is contrary.

EXCEPTIONAL OR NORMAL.

A great deal is said in the Old Testament about the activities of the Holy Spirit. Unless we bear in mind the difference between pre-Christian times and to-day, we may fail to understand them. In the olden times, as we pointed out on pages 21 and 22, the Holy Spirit came *on* certain men. In the case of three (Gideon, for instance: Jugdes vi. 34) the expression is a peculiar one. It really means that the Spirit of the Lord *clothed Himself with* the man in question; He took entire possession of him for a purpose, and until that purpose was effected.

It is the nearest thing that we find in the Old Testament to the filling with the Spirit of which we read so much in the New. But it was always for an exceptional purpose. It was not the normal experience of the chosen instruments on whom the Spirit came.

The same may be said of the Spirit filling John the Baptist, Elisabeth, Zacharias (Luke i. 15, 41, 67), Peter in Acts iv. 8 and Paul in Acts xiii. 9.

But in some cases the filling was normal and continual. Men were *characterised* by being " full of the Holy Ghost." It was so with the seven men in Acts vi. 3 and with Barnabas (Acts xi. 24). It seems also to have been characteristic, for a time at least, of the disciples at Pisidian Antioch (Acts xiii. 52). The exhortation of Ephesians v. 18 places it beyond doubt that it is the will of God that it should be the normal, proper state for every Christian. Alas, how few, comparatively speaking, come up to it !

There is nothing mysterious about it. Ephesians has a great deal to say about the Holy Spirit. The parallel Epistle to the Colossians hardly mentions Him but lays great stress on the personal glory of Christ. Where in Ephesians Paul says : " be filled with the Spirit," in Colossians he says : " Let the word of Christ dwell in you richly " (iii. 16). What does " the word " mean here ? Dr. Moffatt translates : " Let the *inspiration* of Christ dwell in your midst." It amounts to very much the same thing. It is not altogether an individual matter. In our relations one with another the Spirit is to fill and energize us. What is this but the Word of Christ in power and practice?

MORE OF HIM ?

One sometimes hears a Christian say, generally with a sigh, "I know that God has given me His Spirit, but I suppose I need to pray for more of Him."

I do not think that is right. The real reason of our low spiritual condition is not that we want more of the Holy Spirit, but that *He wants more of you and me.*

It is like this. A visitor comes to stay at your house for a few weeks. You treat him courteously and well, but you expect him to confine himself to the part of the house to which you have introduced him.

Now this is not the way the Holy Spirit desires to be treated. He has come to indwell us, not as a mere visitor or guest, but to take charge of the entire establishment of our being, on behalf of Christ. In order that He may do so we must have no reserves with Him, and keep no chambers of the heart locked against Him, but hand over to Him, so to speak, *the key to every room in the house.*

It is of very little moment what name we give to this action. Call it consecration, or entire surrender, or what you will. The name matters little, so long as the reality of the thing is known. But one thing is plain, that in order to be filled with the Holy Ghost we must *allow Him to have undisputed sway over us.*

The crying need of the moment is for men and women with faith to claim and enter upon their God-given privileges. What could not the power of God accomplish through a band of world-emptied, Spirit-filled people ! Reader, neither you nor I can create such a band ; but is it not our bounden duty, as well as our holy privilege, to make sure that we ourselves are such ?

Not that the result of being filled with the Spirit would make us feel that we are wonderful people, who had reached a higher spiritual level than many of our fellow-believers. No indeed !,

The Spirit-filled man is a *Christ-occupied* man, The Holy Ghost's mission is not to occupy us with ourselves, or our state, but to fix the constant gaze of our souls on *Christ.*

So that a Christian who is truly filled by the Holy Ghost would not be found boasting of the fact, or parading it before others. Neither his speech nor his conduct would call attention to himself. He would increasingly realise that he is nothing but a broken and empty vessel, and that all his joy and blessing is in *Christ.* There would, however, be something about him which, unknown to himself, would remind others of *Christ.* He would, unconsciously, leave the savour of *Christ* behind him wherever he went. As to his testimony, it would be with him as with Samuel of old, of whom it is recorded that " the Lord was with him, and did let none of his words fall to the ground " (1 Samuel iii. 19).

THE COMMISSIONER OF THE FATHER.

Besides coming from heaven as the Representative of Christ, the Holy Spirit is here as proceeding from the Father (John xv. 26). One great object of His mission on earth is to form a bride for Christ and bring her to her heavenly Bridegroom. This is beautifully illustrated in the narrative in Genesis xxiv.

When anything is described at length in the Bible, and with great wealth of detail, it is because there is a typical significance in the story. Our attention is called, therefore, to this narrative by the very fact of its length. It fills sixty-seven verses. It will be worth while to refresh the memory by reading the whole chapter before going further.

The story weaves itself around four persons: a father, Abraham; his son, Isaac; an unnamed servant; and the bride, Rebekah.

Abraham typifies God. It is he who sent his trusty servant to find and bring a bride for his son, just as the Father has sent the Holy Spirit, His Commissioner, for this purpose. Isaac, the son, represents Christ. In Chapter xxii he was " received . . . in a figure " (Heb. xi. 19) from the dead, so that he became a foreshadowing of Christ risen.

The servant pictures the Holy Spirit. If he was Eliezer, Abraham's steward forty years previously, the silence of this chapter as to his name is the more remarkable. A name would spoil him as a type of the Holy Spirit. A name calls attention to what anyone is. The Father and the Son have glorious Names, but the Holy Spirit has none. He is here, not to call attention to Himself, nor to present Himself as an Object, but to serve the purposes of the Father concerning the Son.

Rebekah foreshadows the church. Old Testament typology strongly suggests that it is the church, not Israel, nor a remnant of Israel, that is the Bride of Christ. In Revelation xxii. 16 a testimony is given *in the churches*. And it is *there* (in the churches, not in the synagogues) that the voice of the Bride is heard in response. " The Spirit and the Bride say, Come." She speaks with the Spirit, as taught by Him. She has the Holy Spirit, therefore, *before the coming of the Lord.* Israel will not have the Spirit till a future day dawns. Rebekah, the bride, then, represents the Church, the great company of the redeemed from Pentecost till the translation to the Father's house.

THE MISSION OF THE SERVANT.

Seven things are to be noted in connection with the mission on which Abraham's servant (Genesis xxiv) was sent.

1. *The Charge that he received* (verse 4). He was to get a wife for Isaac in the country whither he was sent. Nothing could frustrate this but unwillingness on the part of the maiden. In this case, he would be released from the responsibility of executing his charge. Unwillingness to respond to the call of the Holy Spirit in the gospel prevents one from being saved, and thus sharing in the portion and privileges of the Bride.

2. *The Journey that he took* (verse 10). Abraham had responded to the call of God, but had only gone half-way to the country which God was going to give him. Till his father died, he lived in what is here called the city of Nahor. To this city, representing half-hearted response, the servant went on his mission. Many of us have made but a half-hearted response to God's call. We have appropriated but a small portion of the spiritual territory that He wants us to enjoy. Amongst us has come the Holy Spirit upon His great mission of winning a bride for the heavenly Isaac. Surely this should move and stir us to a more wholehearted response to the call of God that brought us from the land of darkness and death.

3. *The Power that he administered* (verse 10). He took ten camels with him. Would not one, or two or three, have been enough ? Possibly, but the ten set forth the ample power that is at the disposal of the Holy Spirit. These camels were the power by which Rebekah was to be conveyed across the desert. They were not to be used for purposes of self-advertisement or display. If Rebekah had wanted to use them to ride round and exhibit her new jewels and raiment, the servant might have said something like this : " I am not at liberty to permit the camels to be used for any such purpose ; but the moment that you are ready to start on the journey to Isaac, all the ten camels are at your disposal." The whole power of the Holy Spirit is at our back when we pursue the journey that has our glorious Bridegroom as its Goal and Object.

4. *The Testimony that he bore* (verse 36). Speaking of his master's son, he declared : " unto him hath he given all that he hath." In a similar way the Holy Spirit is here testifying to the glory and greatness of Christ, the Appointed Heir of all things. A report of Solomon's glory and wisdom set the Queen of Sheba in movement far away in the south. The report of Isaac's greatness and of his desire for Rebekah made her surroundings unattractive, and she became willing to trust herself to the guidance of the servant, and to start on the journey that led to Isaac. We, too, attracted by the report that has been brought to us of Christ, are no longer held by our surroundings, but have started on the journey that has Himself as its goal.

5. *The Gifts that he brought* (verses 22, 53). These were the Bridegroom's love-gifts. It is well that we think of our blessings thus. But the earring and the bracelets have a further significance. They remind us that our Bridegroom has secured our ears and our hands for Himself: our ears that He may pour into them the story of His love; our hands that we may prove our grateful love to Him by being diligent in His interests.

6. *The Exhortation that he gave* (verse 56): "Hinder me not." It is easy to hinder the Spirit of God having His way with us, by coldness of heart and apathy. It is possible to let our friends hinder. Rebekah's relatives would fain have detained her, if only for a few days. They would have spoiled her immediate and wholehearted response. Have we not heard plausible advice such as: "Avoid Christianity of an extreme kind," "Be moderate in what you do"? If we insist on making a clean break with the world and having only the pleasure of Christ as our motive we shall be misunderstood and derided. Then we have to be on our guard lest by any measure of acquiescence we grieve and hinder the Spirit of God.

7. *The Goal that he reached* (verse 65). The servant conducted Rebekah to Isaac. "And he loved her" (verse 67). The Holy Spirit leads us to Christ, in our affections now, so that we realise something of His love, and it becomes the most precious thing that we possess. Nor will the Holy Spirit desist from His mission until He has brought the Bride in her completeness to the Bridegroom, for Him to present her to Himself (Ephesians v. 27), "a glorious church, not having spot, or wrinkle, or any such thing."

THE CONDUCTOR OF THE SAINT.

Ezekiel, in his vision of glorious things to come, was guided by a man with a measuring line in his hand. Unlike the heavenly messenger that appeared to Daniel (Dan. ix. 21), this man had no name. He is rightly regarded as typifying the Holy Spirit as the One who searches on our behalf the deep things of God that He may lead us into an understanding of them (I Corinthians ii. 10).

He is the Conductor of the saint into God's great and holy things.

The man with the reed appealed to the prophet's eyes, ears and heart (xl. 4). The Holy Spirit desires our wholehearted and undivided attention.

The first thing that Ezekiel beheld and measured was " the breadth " of the building and " the height " (xl. 5), reminding us of how, when we are " strengthened with might by His Spirit in the inner man " it is that, rooted and grounded in love, we " may be able to comprehend with all saints what is the breadth, and length, and depth, and height,"—that is of the counsels and thoughts of God.

Ezekiel's guide shewed him a chamber facing south for certain priests and one facing north intended for those who have a place of special nearness to the Lord (xl. 45, 46). The Holy Spirit would teach us this, that the Lord has sunny places for our souls to dwell in, but that places not so pleasant, places with a northern aspect, facing the quarter from which biting blasts come sweeping down, are sometimes reserved for those who enjoy special intimacy with the Lord. It is part of His gracious discipline.

The guide reveals to the prophet (xliii. 10) the reason why the vision of coming glory was to be shown to the house of Israel. It was not that they might be exhilarated, but that they might be *ashamed*. This is the effect of the disclosures that the Holy Spirit, through the Word, makes to us. Far from ministering to our self-complacency they make us ashamed of ourselves: our coldness, our littleness, our feeble powers of understanding and response. Those truly conducted by the Spirit of God into His deep things are always small in their own eyes.

After leading him out into the unfathomable depths of grace (xlvii. 5) the man with the measuring line conducts Ezekiel back to his starting point which is then a place of fruitbearing. So the Holy Spirit, having made us conversant with great and wonderful things, leads us, here in the world, to bear fruit for Him to whom we belong.

THE CONTROLLER OF THE SERVANTS.

The great landowner, Boaz, the kinsman-redeemer who so strikingly typifies Christ, had a man who represented him on the harvest field, " his servant that was set over the reapers " (Ruth ii. 5). He controlled the young men who did the work. He was in charge of the operations on the field. He is an apt foreshadowing of the Holy Spirit.

He was well acquainted with Ruth's past history and with her desires and exercises. He introduced her to Boaz.

The Holy Spirit knows all the desires and exercises that we have in our souls. Is He not Himself the One who has produced them? And He does us the tremendous service of introducing us to Christ, and fostering our personal acquaintance with Him.

The Holy Spirit represents Christ amid all the activities of the harvest-field. He is set over all the servants, directing, energizing and empowering them in their labours.

We never find in the Scriptures that the servants of Christ are put under a synod, a missionary board, a conference, a committee or an assembly. They are intended to be under the direct control and guidance of the Holy Spirit.

In Acts viii. 29 it was He who bade Philip go and join the chariot of the Ethiopian official. It was He who caught him away from this service to the land of the Philistines.

In Acts xiii. 4 it was the Holy Spirit who sent forth Barnabas and Saul to the island of Cyprus.

He forbade Paul and Silas to preach in the province of Asia. He would not permit them to go into the great province of Bithynia (Acts xvi. 6, 7). Whether sending or forbidding, the Holy Spirit was in direct and plenary control. No human agency or organization intervened, or presumed to receive and pass on His commands to the messengers of Christ.

The elders at Ephesus were such because the Holy Spirit had made them overseers. Their suitability for the office was of His working.

As the servants of the Lord we have to look to Him for guidance. He does indeed guide: but He makes His guidance effectual, and we are enabled to recognize it and obey it, by the Holy Spirit, Christ's true Representative on earth.

THE COMPELLER OF THE SINNER.

The Holy Spirit appears in this character in the Parable of the Great Supper (Luke xiv. 16-23). For of course none but He has the power of compulsion. Preachers may *persuade* men (2 Corinthians v. 11) but only He can *compel*.

Note the outline of the Parable.
1. The Servant is sent with an urgent call to the " many " that had been invited. He carries the announcement that " all things are now ready " and appeals to the invited persons to come.
2. All refuse. It is not that some accept the invitation and other decline. Not one has any desire to attend the feast that grace has provided. *All* make their excuses.
3. The Servant reports this universal refusal, whereupon He is sent to collect poor, crippled and blind persons from the streets and lanes of the city.
4. These, not being enough to fill the house, the Servant is sent yet farther afield, to *compel* men to come in.

The Parable exhibits the difference between free grace and sovereign mercy. Grace addresses everybody, without distinction, and cries " Whosoever will, let him come." But *all* refuse. There is not a soul on earth that naturally desires to share in the great blessings of God. Then sovereign, elective mercy acts. The Holy Spirit works with compelling power in the souls of some (not all), and they are thus constrained to come.

Why the Holy Spirit should work in our hearts, producing conviction of sin and repentance, and not in the hearts of our neighbours, is a mystery of which we have no explanation to offer. But we know that if He had not thus compelled us we should never have come.

In the somewhat similar Parable of the Marriage Feast (Matthew xxii. 1-14) *servants* are sent to gather the guests. They have no power to compel, nor are they infallible. They bring in one whom the King eventually casts out. There is nothing of that kind in the Parable of the Great Supper. Not servants, but the one Servant, is sent forth. He makes no mistakes. None that He brings in are ever cast out. For He works in a way that produces solid and lasting results.

OLD TESTAMENT EMBLEMS,

I. THE DOVE.

The Dove is a well-known emblem of the Holy Spirit, not only because He came upon Christ " in a bodily shape like a dove," but because of what is said of this bird elsewhere in Scripture.

We read of it first in connection with the Deluge (Genesis viii. 6-12). First, Noah sent out a raven. This bird is a type of " the flesh," that evil principle within us, with which we were born into the world. The scene was one of judgment and death, but it was congenial to this unclean creature, and the raven did not return to the ark.

Noah then sent out a dove. There was nothing to attract it, " the dove found no rest for the sole of her foot." It sets forth the condition of the world before Christ came. When He was here, the holy Dove could abide upon Him (John i. 32). But before that, there was no man on whom the Holy Spirit could *rest*. He came upon certain men and empowered them for service. But there were none on whom He could rest.

The second sending out of the dove sets forth what is true at the present time. One thing that had been under the waters of judgment had risen above them. One spot was clear of the judgment, and from that spot the dove brought an olive leaf to Noah. There is to-day one spot that has emerged from under the judgment of God: it is Christ. And because He is free from the load of our guilt and condemnation, we are free too. The Holy Spirit has come down from heaven with the news, and has brought us, as it were, the symbol of peace, the olive leaf, from Christ in glory. " So Noah knew "; and as the result of the testimony which the Holy Spirit bears to the risen Christ, we also may know that our judgment has been borne and our sins put away for ever.

The third sending out of the dove carries our thoughts on to the world to come, the days of the glorious Kingdom which are yet to dawn for this sin-spoiled earth. The scene, cleared by judgment of all that is offensive to God, will then be a congenial abiding place for the Holy Spirit. The renewed earth was a congenial home for the dove; she returned to the ark no more. And in coming days the Holy Spirit will not be given only to those who are " in Christ," but will be poured out *upon all flesh.*

The prediction as to this is found in Joel ii. The Lord will take away the reproach of His people Israel (verse 19); the prosperity of the land will be restored (verses 23-25); " satisfied " will describe the condition of the people (verse 26), and after all this (note the word " afterward " in verse 28) the Lord will pour out His

Spirit upon all flesh. The whole scene will be congenial to the Holy Spirit. What happened at Pentecost was a kind of transient sample of this.

II. THE DEW.

"In the morning the dew lay round about the host. And when the dew that lay was gone up, behold, upon the face of the wilderness there lay a small round thing, as small as the hoar frost on the ground." Exodus xvi. 13, 14.

"And when the dew fell upon the camp in the night, the manna fell upon it." Numbers xi. 9.

The manna is a well-known type of Christ in His earthly life. It was " small ": He made Himself of no reputation. It was " round ": there were no unevennesses of character in Him. It was " white ": His life was one of the whitest purity. It was sweet, " like wafers made with honey ": nowhere is the sweetness of Divine love so manifest as in Him.

Now this " bread from heaven " was only given when the dew lay on the ground in the stillness of the desert night. This dew is an emblem of the Holy Spirit. We are taught, by what is said about it in connection with the manna, that Christ can only be appreciated when the freshness and moisture of the Spirit are in our souls. And this only comes in the stillness of secret communion.

The manna was not appreciated for long by the people of Israel. They soon got tired of it. " Our soul is dried away," they complained, " there is nothing at all, beside this manna, before our eyes." Have we not heard similar language ? " Oh, in that Hall they talk about nothing but Jesus Christ ; we can't go there." " We want life, entertainment, something to make us laugh. We have enough of Jesus Christ on Sundays."

Yes ; it is evident that plenty of people are tired of Christ. One has only to study the subjects chosen for discourses in buildings still called " places *of worship* " to see how widespread is this boredom. But the Holy Spirit is still here. He continues His work of making Christ precious to the hearts of those who heed His ministry. He displaces in their affections the things that once held sway there, and makes a place there for Christ. The result is heavenly freshness and eagerness of soul ; a real desire to know and enjoy more of Christ. The things of the world cease to attract ; Christ becomes an Object of absorbing interest.

Upon such it is manifest that the Dew has fallen. The result is that they enjoy Christ. They feed on Him with delight. Moments spent away from Him are drear and irksome.

III. THE OIL.

With all the Old Testament types of the Holy Spirit there is a greater type of Christ. The type of the Dove is connected with the greater one of the Ark. That of the Dew is overshadowed by that of the Manna. And the Oil stands in manifest connection with the Meat Offering, in which the holy humanity of Christ is set forth typically.

In the old-time ritual of the meat offering (more correctly called the *meal* offering) oil was to be used in a two-fold way. The ordinance is described in Leviticus ii. First, the fine flour that constituted the offering was to be " *mingled with* oil " (verse 6). Secondly oil was to be poured upon it ; the offering was thus to be *anointed*.

The offering itself was to contain no leaven (verse 11). Leaven being invariably in Scripture a symbol of evil (yes, even in Matthew xiii. 33 !), its presence in the meal offering would spoil it as a type of that holy One, in whom was no trace of sin. Neither was the offering to contain honey, for there was no mere natural sweetness in Christ, such as makes us say of a man : " Yes, he's very nice, but ——."

But it was to be mingled with oil. The mingling, it is probable, sets forth the fact that Jesus was " conceived . . . of the Holy Ghost " (Matthew i. 20). He was brought into the world, born of a human mother by the Holy Spirit's power (Luke i. 35). For this reason He, " that holy thing " born of Mary, was called the Son of God. From the very fact and manner of His birth, there was in His substance that which answered to the mingling with oil which made Him, even in His humanity, infinitely more than other men.

The meal offering was subsequently anointed with oil. This undoubtedly finds its fulfilment in what happened to Jesus at His baptism. When the Holy Spirit descended upon Him in bodily shape like a dove, " God anointed Jesus of Nazareth with the Holy Ghost and with power " (Acts x. 38).

Do not let us turn from this study because " there is nothing practical in it for us." Do we not love the Saviour well enough to be interested in all that concerns Him ?

IV. THE RUNNING WATER.

King David, after his great sin, became truly and speedily contrite. Who has not read with emotion his penitential Psalm (the 51st) and echoed his prayer: " Purge me with hyssop, and I shall be clean " ? It was not that David had ceased to be one of God's chosen and loved ones. He had not ceased to trust in and to love the Lord. He had grievously backslidden, however, and needed cleansing.

The cleansing that he needed was not that of a sinner who comes with his lifetime of guilt to the Saviour and receives the cancellation of all that stands against his name in God's book of record. *That* never needs to be repeated. The cleansing that David needed was not cleansing by blood, but cleansing by water, or rather, by what water typified.

No doubt when he prayed to the Lord to purge him with hyssop the ordinance of the Red Heifer (Numbers xix) was in his mind. A red heifer without blemish was to be slain and burned. The ashes were to be laid up in a clean place till needed. The need arose when one came in contact with any defiling thing, such as a dead body, a human bone, or a grave (verse 16). The ashes were to be applied to the defiled person by means of *running water*. Hyssop was to be dipped in the water into which the ashes had been cast and sprinkled on the person concerned.

The death of Christ (represented by the ashes, the result of sacrifice) has to be applied, not as an atonement for guilt, but as that which morally cleanses the mind and heart from the defilement which a believer contracts. The running water is an emblem of the Holy Spirit, for it is He who brings the death of Christ to bear upon our souls. He uses it as a lever to move us to self-judgment and thus to bring about our cleansing and restoration.

How easily we may contract defilement! "Every open vessel, which hath no covering bound upon it, is unclean" (verse 15). We are surrounded by contaminating influences. If we fail to keep a covering upon our souls, we shall be polluted. What is the covering that will preserve us? A season of prayer and communion with God each day before we go forth to mix with others.

V. THE SPRINGING WELL.

Four things in Numbers xxi seem purposely put together. (1) The Serpent of brass, portraying Christ uplifted on the Cross for us so that we may look to Him and have life. (2) The Sunrising, towards which the people of Israel pitched after leaving Oboth (verse 11). We may pitch in the opposite direction, and be always discontented and gloomy. Or we may pitch toward the sunrising and have our souls filled with the very gladness of heaven. (3) The Springing Well, and with it (4) The Song.

The Springing Well sets forth the energy of the Holy Spirit within our souls for joy and worship. It was of this that the Lord spoke to the Samaritan woman. He not only presented Himself as the Source from which "living water" might be obtained, but spoke of a well of water *in* the one who drinks thereof, springing up. Both the rivers flowing out (John vii. 38) and the well springing up (John iv. 14) typify the power of the Holy Spirit. The springing well sets forth His power and energy for worship. The flowing rivers set forth His power and energy for service and testimony.

What is the worship that the Holy Spirit produces and energises ? It is something produced *within*. No worship is real unless it comes from the heart. I may be one of a congregation assembled in some " place of worship." I may bow my head reverently while praise is offered to God. I may join in singing the hymns. But this does not constitute me a worshipper in spirit and in truth. It is only what the Holy Spirit forms in the heart, and that wells up in gratitude and joy, that is worship in the true sense.

Our poverty of worship springs from the fact that we do not habitually pitch toward the sunrising. Alexander the Great had a valuable horse which he named Bucephalus. It was terribly afraid of its own shadow and could only be calmed and tamed by turning its head towards the sun. Then, of course, its shadow was behind it, and could no longer be seen.

What a different tone our worship would have if we more constantly turned towards our Sun, and opened our hearts to all that He has revealed Himself to be in His eternal love. There would be less talking about ourselves and our blessings, for we should be more occupied with the Father and His beloved Son.

THE SEVEN SPIRITS OF GOD.

This strange phrase, which occurs four times in the Revelation, has puzzled many. " Is there more than one Holy Spirit ? " they have asked.

Of course there is only one Holy Spirit. "There is one body, and ONE Spirit" (Ephes. iv. 4). The Book of Revelation itself, in which the mysterious words occur, teaches the unity of the Person of the Spirit. "I was in the Spirit," says John (i. 10). "The Spirit and the bride say, Come" (xxii. 17).

The Revelation is a symbolic Book and many things are said which are not to be interpreted as statements of literal truth. Christ is spoken of under the figure of a lamb with seven horns and seven eyes. Nobody would fail to see that this is wholly figurative. We must remember this in connection with the words that stand at the head of this chapter. No one, we hope, imagines that there are seven Holy Spirits. There is only one.

But if the language be figurative, it is a figurative of something, and in explaining it we must be careful not to explain it *away*, and to rob the words of all meaning. What, then, are we to learn from what we read as to the Seven Spirits of God?

Seven is itself a symbolic number and is so used in the Revelation as conveying the idea of completeness. In John's visions there were seven candle-sticks, seven seals, seven trumpets, seven vials, seven thunders, etc. "Seven Spirits of God" is a phrase that expresses the idea of a complete cycle of Divine activities, just as the seven trumpets express the idea of a complete cycle of Divine judgments.

In Revelation i. 4 the "seven Spirits" are mentioned as being before the throne, the centre of Divine administration, whether of blessing or of judgment. Their connection in this passage with "Him which is, and which was, and which is to come" suggests a dispensational interpretation, a reference to the activities of the

Holy Spirit in present, past and future. To this matter we will return later.

In Revelation iii. 1 " the seven Spirits of God " are brought in in connection with Christ's administration in the churches, and administration carried out through the plenary power of the Spirit.

In Revelation iv. 5 the seven lamps of fire (symbols of judgment) are interpreted as signifying the seven Spirits of God. The adminstration of judgment is also effected in the fulness of His power.

Lastly, in Revelation v. 6 the seven Spirits of God are found in connection with the Lamb's administration of the whole earth, which will be actually brought to pass in a future age.

THE SEVEN SPIRITS OF GOD.
(Dispensational Interpretation.)

I have suggested a dispensational interpretation of the Seven Spirits before the throne in Revelation i. 4. They might be enumerated as follows.

1. THE SPIRIT OF CREATIVE ENERGY.
Genesis i. 2.

At the beginning, when " the deep " had been formed and darkness was still upon its surface, " the Spirit of God moved upon the face of the waters." The word " moved " conveys the idea of intense activity. The import of the passage is lost if it be changed to "brooded." A brooding hen is still and quiet, while in Genesis i. 2 activity is the thought suggested.

The Spirit of God was there to give effect to the Word of God. By His Word God created the universe ; He made His Word effectual by His Spirit.

"God *said*, Let there be a firmament"; that was the fiat of His Word. "And God *made* the firmament"; that was the work of His Spirit. "God said" and "God made" are the keywords of the creation narrative His Word is made effectual by the working of the Spirit.

It is the same in spiritual things. The Word and the Spirit, as we saw on pages 31 and 32, are the means by which the new birth is brought to pass.

The shining of light is not enough to produce a photograph on a glass plate. The plate must be sensitized so that the impression may be received. The light comes to us by the Gospel, the Word of God. Our souls, sensitized, wrought upon, convicted, by the work of the Holy Spirit, receive that Word and we are born anew.

"God said, Let there be lights in the firmament of the heaven." What part had the Spirit in that? Job tells us. "By His Spirit He hath garnished the heavens" (Job xxvii. 13). When God spake, His Spirit, the Spirit of creative energy, was there in mighty activity to make the Word of God effectual. We may use this as an illustration of spiritual things, but it remains a fact of primeval history that the Spirit of God wrought thus.

2. THE SPIRIT OF RESTRAINT.

Genesis vi. 3.

We may gather that ever since the fall of our first parents as the result of their temptation in the Garden of Eden, the Spirit of God had been striving with men.

This had gone on for a period of some fifteen hundred years.

In spite of all the striving of Him whom, in this connection, we have called the Spirit of restraint, men filled the earth with violence and wickedness. This could not go on for ever, and God declared : " My Spirit shall not always strive with man."

I do not deny that the Holy Spirit strives with sinners to-day. I have touched on this subject on pages 58 and 59. But it is not the *characteristic* activity of the Spirit in these days, as it was before the Flood. The Flood was the end of the age when the Holy Spirit, as the Spirit of restraint, wrought to check the increasing wickedness and strove with men to keep them from carrying out their evil designs.

Some have taken the concluding clause of Genesis vi. 3 to mean that man's age was from that point limited to 120 years. But men lived to be older than that for a long time. Noah was 950 when he died. Abraham was 175. Miriam was well over 120. Job lived 140 years *after his trial*.

It is more probable, therefore, that the 120 years mentioned referred to the time during which the Holy Spirit would continue to strive with men. After that, the longsuffering and patience of God would give place to wrath, and the Deluge would come upon the world.

The Spirit of Restraint does not work in the same way to-day, for three times in Romans i, in that terrible account of the world that had broken loose from the will of its Creator, we read : " God gave them up," " God also gave them up," " God gave them over." Not as the Spirit of Restraint, but as the Spirit of Grace, He works to-day.

When men persisted in their rebellion, and crucified the Saviour, then, in virtue of the great sacrifice of Calvary, God offered His undeserved pardon, and the Holy Spirit works to make this effectual.

3. THE SPIRIT OF PROPHECY AND INSPIRATION.

Whether in the earliest days of human history any revelation of God to men was recorded on clay tablets, or in any other way, we do not know. If so, such writings have not been preserved for us, though it is possible that a passage such as we have in Jude 14, 15 is a quotation from an antediluvian document.

But after about a third of the period of human history had gone by, the Holy Spirit began to move men to *write*. Moses was the first to be thus inspired. He was followed by others, notably David, several of the Prophets, and Ezra. Some, like Elijah and Elisha were inspired to prophesy, but not to write.

The Spirit of Christ, that is, the Spirit who testified to the future sufferings and subsequent glory of Christ, was in these ancient servants of God as the Spirit of prophecy and inspiration (1 Peter i. 11, 12). They " spake as they were moved by the Holy Ghost " (2 Peter i. 21). That word " moved " is a word used in connection with navigation to describe how ships are carried along by the breeze. Holy men of God were " carried along " by the Spirit of prophecy and inspiration.

This fact gives character to the writings of the Old Testament. We learn from Acts i. 16 that the selfsame

Holy Spirit for whom the disciples were waiting, and who came at Pentecost, was the One who spoke by the mouth of David in the Psalms. Let us avoid thinking of the Old Testament as a mere collection of Hebrew religious books. After quoting from the ninety-fifth Psalm, the writer of the Epistle to the Hebrews speaks of it as the Word (logos) of God, and tells us that it is *quick* (that is, living) and powerful (Hebrews iv. 12).

The Old Testament has a wonderful power to search the conscience. Through its pages we learn to have to do with God.

The Lord asked His disciples : " Have ye understood all these things ? " (Matthew xiii. 51). They answered " Yea, Lord." But the proof of their understanding would be that they would be able to bring forth from their treasure (of knowledge) things new *and old*. True wisdom would never discard the Old. It would possess fresh value because of the New. Men of understanding would " bring forth the old because of the new " (Leviticus xxvi. 10). Both alike are the work of the Holy Spirit.

4. THE SPIRIT OF HOLINESS.

We now come to the period covered by the life and ministry of the Son of God on earth. He who wrought at the beginning, as the Spirit of Creative Energy, to form an arena for the display of God's wisdom and power, was now going to work for the bringing into being of another creation, wherein God would be known in holy love, and in the fruition of all the bright designs of His grace.

The Spirit of holiness marked out Jesus as the Son of God by the resurrection of (the) dead, that is, by His raising of dead persons. There can, I think, be no doubt that this is the meaning of Romans i. 4. See Darby's "New Translation" and the marginal note in the Scofield Bible. There is in the Greek no article before the word for dead, and this word is in the genitive plural. It cannot refer to one person, but to many. The literal English rending is " of dead " (plural); that is, of dead persons.

When the Lord went to Bethany to raise Lazarus from the tomb, it was " that *the Son of God* might be glorified thereby " (John xi. 4). He also raised the little daughter of Jairus and the son of the widow of Nain. But these were by no means all. It was *characteristic* of the ministry of Christ on earth, not only that " the blind receive their sight and the lame walk ; the lepers are cleansed and the deaf hear " but that " *the dead are raised up* " (Matthew xi. 5).

We need not exclude from the passage the thought of Christ's own resurrection. But the point is that the Spirit of holiness, who wrought, and is still working, to bring us in our thoughts and affections already, as actually by-and-by, to a world of holiness, love and perfection, established in resurrection, marked out Christ as the One who should establish that world. He Himself was Resurrection and Life when He was here (John xi. 25), and as the Son He quickened whom He would (John v. 21), whether physically or spiritually.

It is a great thing for our souls to get hold of, that all God's thoughts of blessing are brought to pass in a world that is based on resurrection. Christ, the

First-born from the dead, is the Beginning of that "creation of God" (Rev. iii. 14), and the Spirit of holiness marked Him out as the Son of God in that He, and He alone, has power to bring others into that resurrection world, to share its joys with Him.

5. THE SPIRIT OF GRACE.

This chapter brings us to what characterises the Holy Spirit in this period in which our lot is cast.

As the Spirit of Grace (Hebrews x. 29) He works in six principal ways.

(i) *Preaching the Gospel.* Those who proclaim the glad tidings of salvation do so "with the Holy Ghost sent down from heaven" (1 Peter i. 12). He is behind every true evangelistic enterprise. He moves the servants of Christ to carry the good news far and wide; to cross the seas and declare "the Gospel of the Grace of God" in China, India, Africa and many a distant land. To preach without the Holy Spirit is to labour in vain. One's preaching is futile and powerless.

(ii) *Begetting us anew.* He works with the Word to produce in our hearts a response, so that, believing the Gospel we are born anew, or born "from above." This is the Holy Spirit's work in grace. We are "born of the Spirit" (John iii. 6).

(iii) *Compelling to come in* (Luke xiv. 23). We have spoken on pages 91 and 92 of this gracious activity of the Spirit of God, so need not repeat.

(iv) *Bearing witness to us,* that our sins and iniquities are remembered by God no more (Hebrews x. 15-17).

This subject is dealt with in detail in the chapters entitled "The Witness."

(v) *Shedding God's love abroad* in our hearts (Romans v. 5). In the early chapters of Romans great stress is laid on righteousness. God's righteousness is revealed in the Gospel (i. 17); righteousness of God is offered to all through faith in Christ (iii. 22); to him who believes God imputes righteousness without works (iv. 5). Now righteousness, necessary as it is, does not stir and warm the heart like love. It is as if the Apostle said: "The Gospel is not *all* righteousness; there is love as well. And the Holy Spirit, given to us, makes us conscious of God's great love: He sheds it abroad in our hearts."

(vi) *Empowering the servants of the Lord* (Acts i. 8). It is the power of the Holy Spirit alone that enables any of us to bear our share in the propaganda committed by the Lord to His servants.

6. THE SPIRIT OF JUDGMENT.

When the present day of grace comes to an end, and those who are Christ's are translated to be with Himself, the Holy Spirit, though no longer Resident on earth in the same way as now, will continue to work for the bringing to pass of the Divine purposes. But on what different lines will He work then!

Not as the Spirit of grace in an arena wide as the world, but in Israel, especially in Jerusalem, as the Spirit of Judgment (Isaiah iv. 4). The servants of God who witness for Him in that day will be as " olive trees "

(Rev. xi. 4), that is, filled with the Spirit (compare Zechariah iv. 1-6), but, as with Micah in by-gone days, it will not be the Spirit of *grace*. They will be " full of power by the Spirit of the Lord, and *of judgment*, and of might " (Micah iii. 8).

As the Spirit of Judgment He will work by fire and burning to cleanse away the filth of His people of Israel and to bring in the glorious condition described in Isaiah iv. 4-6.

I was watching a man painting a gate. He had a lamp, the flame of which was directed forward. He held this against the old, dirty paint, scorching and blistering it. Then with the sharp edge of a tool he scraped it off. All this had an ultimate purpose in view. He was preparing the gate, by flame and burning, for the application of the new paint.

Similarly the Spirit of Judgment will work by " burning," removing all that is evil, in order that the way may be prepared for the establishment in glory of the Kingdom of Christ.

7. THE SPIRIT OF EARTH-WIDE BLESSING.

This is what the Holy Spirit will be in the days that usher in the glory of the Millennial reign of Christ. He will be poured out on all flesh, Jew and Gentile alike (Joel ii. 28). We need enter into no detail here, as reference is made to this future activity of the Spirit on pages 53, 54, 92 and 93.

THE LAYING ON OF HANDS.

A belief is entertained in some quarters that the laying on of hands is necessary, both for the reception of the Holy Spirit and for recognition as a Christian minister. Hence the Confirmation and Ordination services in the English State Church.

As to the claims of " bishops " to ordain the servants of Christ, I may be permitted to refer the reader to my previous book, " Royal Service : a Study in Christian Leadership." Our present concern is as to what the New Testament says about the laying on of hands in connection with the reception of the Holy Spirit.

We find two, and only two, instances of it. In every other case recorded, there is no mention of any human intervention. In Acts x. 44 the Holy Spirit was given while the recipients were hearing Peter preach ; there was no laying on of hands, In Acts xiii. 52 the disciples were filled with joy and with the Holy Spirit ; again, no laying on of hands. The fact that in only two cases there was the laying on of *apostolic* (not episcopal) hands should lead us to conclude that this was the exceptional, not the usual, means whereby God bestowed the Holy Spirit upon believing men and women.

The first exception to the general rule was in the case of the Samaritans (Acts viii. 15-17). These people had the microbe of independence in their blood. They had a Samaritan Bible, a Samaritan holy mountain and a Samaritan temple. No doubt they would have liked to have had a Samaritan church and a Samaritan Holy Spirit.

This would have introduced a breach into the unity of Christianity, and we recognize the wisdom of God in preventing it by an unusual procedure. There was to be one body, one Spirit, one Lord, one faith, one baptism ; so God did not permit the Samaritan believers to receive the Holy Spirit apart from the church at Jerusalem, where Christianity had already been established. They had to wait till " the apostles *which were at*

Jerusalem" could send two of their number. Thus was the link formed, and the unity of the Spirit kept.

These actual conditions were not perpetuated; there was no further occasion for exceptional procedure. No doubt in all future cases of conversion among the Samaritans each believer received the Holy Spirit as the gift of God directly on his putting his faith in the Saviour, just as those who believe to-day receive Him.

" HAVE YE RECEIVED THE HOLY GHOST ? "

The only other case of the Holy Spirit being bestowed with the laying on of apostolic hands is that of the twelve men at Ephesus, recorded in Acts xix. 1-8. An examination of this incident will enable us at the same time to answer a question that is sometimes asked: " Do we not read of some who believed, and who yet had not received the Holy Spirit ? " The questioner often bases his enquiry on this narrative.

Our reply is that these twelve men are not said to have believed the Gospel of their salvation. How could they believe what they had never heard ? What they *had* heard was the message which John the Baptist was sent to proclaim: repentance, in view of the coming of the Kingdom of God. Receiving this message, they had been baptized unto John's baptism, and they seem to have received no further light till Paul visited their city.

Paul could preach what John the Baptist could not, namely, redemption accomplished through the blood of Christ; the work all finished; Christ risen from the dead; forgiveness and salvation offered freely in His name to every creature. This was indeed the Gospel of their salvation, and these very men were among those who are reminded later on that it was when they had believed *that* they were sealed with the Holy Spirit.

But why should Paul have laid his hands on them? To understand the reason we must remember that John the Baptist, even after the Lord had begun to gather disciples, had *disciples of his own*. These did not adhere to Christ though they found in Him a sympathetic Friend (Matthew xiv. 12). John's mission was intended to be introductory: it threatened to be permanent. The organization spread. It reached Egypt and had its representatives in Ephesus, it had become in a way a rival to Christianity.

The twelve men at Ephesus were in this position. On hearing the Gospel from the lips of Paul they received it, declaring their faith by submitting to Christian baptism. The bond of fellowship with these newcomers on true Christian ground was recognised and ratified by the Apostle by his laying hands on them. It was like the case of the Samaritan believers, an exceptional procedure, and must not be regarded as a precedent to be followed to-day, especially on the part of men who are certainly not Apostles.

THE WITNESS.

Old Mr. Wesley lay dying. His famous sons, John and Charles, were at his bedside. Turning to John, he said: "The inward witness, my son, that is the proof, the strongest proof of Christianity."

Arnold Lunn, in his book on John Wesley, calls this " a phrase which was destined to play a great role in Methodism." It has indeed done so.

My father, the late William Barker, was a much-used evangelist in his day, lived for years in Cornwall, and was continually in contact with Methodists of all kinds, many of them saintly men and women, whose lives bore eloquent testimony to the transforming power of Christ.

" The witness of the Spirit " was a phrase frequently on their lips. Some were ardently praying for it ; others claimed to have received it. All agreed that, whether they possessed it or not, it is something that expresses itself in happy feelings, exalted spiritual experiences, inward persuasions that one is in " a state of grace." In order to meet this misleading notion my father wrote a booklet on the subject, which was widely circulated all over the area in which he laboured. It was the means of emancipating many from an idea that involved them in endless variations of confidence, ranging from ecstatic assurance to deep despondency.

" I, who went to America to convert others, was never myself converted to God," wrote John Wesley. He was probably right. But how came he to know that he was converted at length ? He based his assurance on certain feelings that came to him while attending a meeting at Aldersgate Street, London. This, he supposed, was the Spirit witnessing to him of his acceptance with God.

Old-fashioned Methodism is not yet extinct, though a new race of Methodist ministers, who have dropped the word " conversion " from their theology, is responsible for destroying it in many quarters. But questions are still asked, and the souls of people are still exercised, as to the great question of one's personal relations with God.

It is hoped that such may be helped by what follows. My father's booklet is better than anything that I can write on the subject, and I reproduce it as part of this larger book. The whole subject of the Spirit's witness is of great practical importance though woefully misunderstood.

THE WITNESS: WHAT IS IT?

What are we to understand by the Witness of the Spirit about which some Christian people talk so much? The Scriptures speak of it; and earnest souls, not a few, with vague and mistaken notions of its meaning, have been known to long for it anxiously and almost hopelessly, for many a weary year. But the question is, what does it mean?

Many have undertaken to answer this enquiry, and definitions have been handed down to us bearing the names of dear and honoured men. To these we listen with attention and respect, but at the same time plead the right to test their teaching by the Word of God, even as the Bereans, when Paul himself preached to them (Acts xvii. 10, 11).

One tells us that the witness of the Spirit is an inward impression of the soul, whereby the Spirit of God directly witnesses to us that all our sins are blotted out. A second voice declares that the witness of the Spirit is seen in our loving, delighting in, and rejoicing in God; so that the humble Christian, perceiving these graces in himself, no longer doubts his acceptance, or his being a child of God. In keeping with this, another exhorts to careful self-examination, to see whether these marks of God's children are borne by us or not.

One thing seems certain, that all such explanations of the witness of the Spirit, quite apart from their being true or false, tend to turn the mental eye in upon self, and lead us to conclude whether we are saved or not by what we chance to discover there. Oft-times, if the truth be told, the result is sufficiently dark and dismal ; and when otherwise it is clear that no enduring peace of mind can flow from this process of introspection, for where shall one be found whose inward spiritual state is every day alike ?

Hence numbers who entertain these views think themselves saved one day, and doubt it the next. If satisfied with what goes on within, they are almost in an ecstasy ; and if not, they are almost in despair. I speak now of earnest, upright souls. In their brighter moments they suppose the Spirit is witnessing to them their interest in Christ ; in their darker ones, that the gracious witness is wanting. Now all this, we make bold to say, betrays a lack of understanding what the witness of the Spirit really is.

THE WITNESS: A COMMON MISTAKE.

Let me suppose myself speaking to one of this class. I ask of him the plain question, " Are your sins forgiven ?" He replies in the affirmative. I tell him I am rejoiced to hear it, and beg him to inform me how he became assured of this consoling fact. The answer · I receive amounts to this, that his assurance proceeds from a careful examination of the state of his own heart and of his experiences. He has been blessed of late with many happy frames of feeling and, putting all things together, he believes that he may humbly conclude that he is a subject of divine favour. Indeed, he is firmly persuaded these happy frames can be nothing else than the Holy Spirit witnessing to him that he is in a state of grace.

Whereupon I venture to enquire whether it is always thus with him, and learn, alas! that it is not. Would that it were! Sometimes the evidences are not so clear. Love to God languishes, the heart grows cold, there is but little liberty in prayer, and he fears he has grieved the Holy Spirit away. Downcast and desponding, he is ready to think that he has fallen from grace, and is in a sad state.

The only rejoinder I am able to make to my imaginary friend is this: "Dear sir, if I mistake not, you confound things that differ. You are looking for the effects of the Spirit in you, the effects of being born again, instead of resting by faith on the blood-shedding, death, resurrection, and ascension of the Lord Jesus Christ for pardon and acceptance with God. Moreover, you draw what assurance of salvation you happen to have from happy feelings and experiences instead of the sure testimony of God's Word, by which the believer in Jesus may always know that he is forgiven and saved. In fact, the witness of the Spirit is the very thing you have *not* yet received."

Should answer be made, "Nay; I do believe that Jesus is the Son of God, and I have no hope outside His atonement; but I search my own heart to see if in truth I have an interest in Christ, or am only deceiving myself. Surely I am right in doing this. If I have an interest in Christ shall I not feel happy? And you certainly would not wish me to be content without such assuring experiences." To that I say, If you believe in Jesus you *are* forgiven, you *are* justified from all things. (Acts xiii. 38, 39.) God testifies to that fact in His Word, and not to believe Him is a sad sin. When God speaks, shall I say: "O God, Thou hast spoken, but I dare not believe what Thou sayest, unless my feelings assure me of the truth of Thy Word"?

THE WITNESS:
A MISTAKE CORRECTED.

It is sometimes said: "St. Paul exhorts us to examine ourselves, to see whether we are in the faith. Are we not, then, to do so?"

I reply, the use you make of Paul's words in 2 Corinthians xiii. 3-5 shows that you have mistaken his meaning altogether. Let me quote the verses, omitting the words that come in by the way, so that the connection may be more easily seen. "Since ye seek a proof of Christ speaking in me . . . . examine yourselves, whether ye be in the faith; prove your own selves. Know ye not your own selves, how that Jesus Christ is in you, except ye be reprobates?" The Corinthians, though converted by the apostle's ministry, had nevertheless lent their ear to his traducers. They went so far as to actually demand proofs of Paul that Christ spoke in him. "Do you require proofs?" said he, in answer to their demand. "What better proofs can you have than yourselves? Search and see. Are you Christians? Are you standing in the Christian faith? Is Jesus Christ really in you? If so, how did it come about? By whose means?" There could be but one answer. It was by Paul's preaching they had been brought into the blessings of the Gospel. Then they themselves were the most convincing proof that Christ did speak through him. This they must acknowledge unless they were willing to confess themselves reprobates. The argument of the apostle furnishes no warrant whatever for the practice for which you plead.

But let us see exactly what the witness of the Spirit is. Turn to Hebrews x. and read verses 15, 16 and 17: "Whereof the Holy Ghost also is a witness to us: for after that He had said before, This is the covenant that I will make with them after those days, saith the Lord ; I will put My laws into their hearts, and in their minds will I write them ; and their sins and iniquities will I remember no more."

Two things are evident from this passage. First, that the Holy Spirit Himself takes the place of a witness. Secondly, what the witness is which the Holy Spirit bears.

In everyday affairs the difference between a witness himself and the witness he bears is easily perceived. Suppose you were called to give evidence in a court of justice. The day comes when the case is to be heard, and you take your place among the witnesses. When called into the witness-box you state what you know, and what you state is your witness. So in this passage the Holy Spirit is the Witness, and the witness He bears is expressed, as yours would be, in simple human speech.

THE WITNESS:
THE PERSON AND HIS TESTIMONY.

Think of the Holy Spirit being a Witness ! Here is one greater than Gabriel, greater than all the angels put together, One whose word is as far above theirs as the Creator is above the creature. Could you have a more honourable witness than the Holy Ghost ? a more trustworthy one than the Spirit of Truth ? If *He* testifies, then beyond all doubt His testimony is true ; if *He* bears witness, then His words cannot be shaken, they may be received without reserve. The witness of the Spirit is indeed a firm foundation for our faith. A firmer could not be found either in heaven or on earth.

Advance a step further. What is it that the Spirit witnesses ? In answering this question keep in mind that one of the chief points in Hebrews ix. and x. is the clearing of the conscience from the pressure and burden of sins. The writer argues that the sacrifices offered on Jewish altars never accomplished that. Whatever measure of relief they gave, it was impossible that they should purge the conscience. Even the great sacrifices of the day of atonement brought the people's sins to remembrance, and shewed that there was no settlement *once for all* of the solemn question of sins and guilt. (Hebrews x. 3.)

But when the epistle to the Hebrews was written the Great Sacrifice had been offered. Precious atoning blood had been shed, whose efficacy remains in undiminished force. Shall no richer results flow from this than had flowed from Jewish sacrifices ? Shall uneasiness and uncertainty and a burdened conscience be the portion of those who are under the shelter of the blood of Christ ? Impossible ! " By one offering He hath perfected for ever them that are sanctified, whereof the Holy Ghost also is a witness to us." (Heb. x. 14, 15.) *Perfected for ever* ! Wonderful words ! The question of sins never to be raised again, settled, set at rest for evermore. Such is the testimony this chapter bears. Let the reader ponder it well.

Then follows the distinct and confirmatory witness of the Holy Ghost, a witness borne in words of marvellous plainness. It is drawn from Jeremiah xxxi. 33, 34, and is quoted more particularly for the sake of its concluding words. What are those words ? What is the witness which this Divine Witness bears ? Listen to it ! for ear never heard anything more sweet, more blessed. This is it, " THEIR SINS AND INIQUITIES WILL I REMEMBER NO MORE." Did ever witness in earthly courts bear clearer, brighter testimony than that ?

THE WITNESS: NOTHING MYSTERIOUS.

The witness of the Holy Spirit is nothing vague, mysterious, and hard to be explained. It is a *spoken* witness, a *written* witness, and, thank God, it is not written in such uncertain, changing characters as frames and feelings, which assume one form to-day and another to-morrow. The witness of the Spirit is fixed and unvarying; it is inscribed on the imperishable pages of that living Book of God which we call the Bible; it is *there* the Spirit witnesseth to us that our sins and iniquities God will remember *no* more.

He will remember them *no more*. They have been remembered, all of them little and great. Every sin of your earthly history, from childhood to youth, from youth to manhood, from manhood to old age; in short, every sin has come up in remembrance before God. Do any ask, When? Where? I answer, At Calvary. There the Saviour suffered for them, the Just for the unjust. There God remembered them, and dealt with Him about them. Therefore does the Holy Ghost witness that they shall be remembered *no more*.

And now, wherever a Bible is found, by day and by night, on land and sea, in spring and summer, autumn and winter, in the valleys and on the hills, amid the rush of business and the quiet of home, in sickness and health, in dark days and bright, in seasons of doubt and of unshaken faith, always and under all circumstances the Holy Spirit is bearing witness to this stupendous fact, that our sins and iniquities God will remember *no more*.

To all believers alike, the youngest and oldest, the faultiest and the most perfect, the most miserable and the most rejoicing, is this blessed testimony borne.

It knows no ups and downs, it changes not, it varies not, nor is it ever withdrawn, but is always the same, yesterday, to-day, and for ever.

What shall be done with this witness of the Spirit? or, rather, what *should* be done with it? Shall we discredit it, view it with suspicion, hesitate to receive it, as something too simple, too great, too blessed to be true? God forbid! That would be a poor return for grace so great. One thing only should be done with it: *it should be believed.*

And wherever this witness is believed, there perfect peace as to the forgiveness of sins is known and enjoyed. These things cannot be separated, for the one follows the other as surely as effects follow cause. You could no more receive the witness of the Spirit and not have quietness of mind as to your sins, than you could throw open the shutters of a dark room and the light not stream in.

THE WITNESS: "TO" AND "WITH."

By the once offered Sacrifice of Calvary our sins are taken from the conscience, or, as it is expressed in Hebrews x. 2, we have "no more conscience of sins." The precious blood of Christ removes them from under the eye of God; and the witness of the Spirit, that therefore God will remember them no more, if believed, takes the condemning load off the conscience.

There are numbers whose sins are gone from God's sight, but not from their conscience. If I owe a debt and cannot pay it I do not like to meet my creditor. Suppose some one pays it for me, but never tells me a word about it, the debt is still on my conscience, and troubles me though it has been paid. I need not only to have the debt paid, but also to know that it has been. The one offering of Christ on the cross is the payment, and the witness of the Holy Ghost is to let me know that it is all settled. " Their sins and iniquities will I remember no more." Blessed testimony ! May each reader receive it !

But there is a passage in Romans viii. which deals with the witness of the Spirit in a somewhat different way. Let me quote it : " The Spirit itself beareth witness with our spirit, that we are the children of God." (Rom. viii. 16.)

The witness borne here is not the same as in Hebrews x. 17. It may help the reader to discern the difference if he observes that in Hebrews x. the Spirit witnesses *to us*, while in Romans the Spirit witnesses *with* our spirit. Moreover, in the former case, as I trust we have amply shewn, the Spirit's witness is to the effect that our sins and iniquities God will remember no more ; but in the latter the Spirit witnesseth with our spirit that we are God's children. Now that God should fully and freely forgive is one thing ; but it is quite another that He should make the forgiven one His child.

It is a remarkable fact in connection with the subject we are discussing that the Holy Spirit is never named in the Epistle to the Romans, except incidentally in Chapter i. 4, till Chapter v. is reached. This silence is significant. God would not have us confound, or mix up, the Spirit's work with the atoning work of Christ. Therefore we find no unfolding of the Spirit's place and work until we arrive at chapter viii., and then they are largely dealt with.

But we shall have more to say about this in our next chapter.

THE WITNESS: WITH OUR SPIRIT.

If the Epistle to the Romans be read in order, it will be seen that long before we reach Chapter viii., the chapter that has so much to say about the Holy Spirit, everything relating to our sins has been settled, so that the believer is declared to be justified, at peace with God, standing in divine favour, and rejoicing in hope of God's glory, ere the Spirit is even once named. (Rom. v. 1,2.) Nor have our experiences any mention either. The death and resurrection of the Lord Jesus are the great *facts* set before our eyes; and we, believing in the efficacy of the blood of Christ, in Him too who is the Justifier of the ungodly, and who raised up Jesus our Lord from the dead, are blessed in the way so beautifully unfolded in the first two verses of Romans v.

It is undoubtedly an immense thing to be forgiven, and to know it on divine authority, by the witness borne in words by the Holy Ghost; yet the grace of God cannot be measured by forgiveness of sins only. It goes much further. Those who are forgiven are also His children, being born of Him. Having faith in Christ, they are owned too as sons. In the great charter of the believer's privileges, the fact of his sonship is plainly written down. Is he not to know it ? Assuredly he is, and to know it in power too.

The believer, knowing that he is a child of God, finds the feelings and affections of his new nature go out towards God his Father. But not only does his own renewed spirit thus bear witness that he is a child, but the indwelling Holy Spirit also witnesses with his spirit that he is indeed a child of God. Up to this point in the epistle the believer has been viewed in no such relationship. Saint and servant he has been said to be, but there has been no reference to his being a child. He is now plainly declared to be one, and the Spirit he has received enables him to cry, Abba. Such is the witness of the Spirit in Romans viii. 16.

However much the Spirit may be grieved, and have to occupy the believer with his ways, so as to lead him to confession and self-judgment, when he has failed, and got out of communion with God, He never leads him to doubt either his forgiveness or his relationship with God as His child. Would the Spirit ever lead us to doubt the value of the blood of Christ, to discredit the witness He Himself has given, or to question that relationship of which He Himself is proof ? Never !

THE WITNESS: ETERNAL LIFE.

Before we close our study of this important subject, there remains yet another passage to be examined, in which the witness of the Spirit finds a place : 1 John v. 6-13. Here it stands in other connections still. It is not here the Holy Spirit witnessing to us that our sins and iniquities shall be remembered no more, nor is it the Spirit witnessing with our spirit that we are the children of God. The witness here is to the immense truth that God has given unto us *eternal life*, and that this life is in His Son.

" There are three that bear witness on earth, the Spirit, and the water, and the blood "—three witnesses, but one testimony. These three witness on God's behalf that eternal life is ours.

" He that believeth on the Son of God hath the witness in himself." What does this mean ? Why, that the

Holy Spirit Himself dwells in the body of the believer. " What ? know ye not that your body is the temple of the Holy Ghost which is *in you* ? " (1 Cor. vi. 19.) The believer, being born again and cleansed by the precious blood of Christ, is sealed with that Holy Spirit of promise: and the Spirit thus given is the witness to him that eternal life is his as well as the earnest of what he shall inherit in that day of coming glory. (Eph. i. 13.)

The blood and the water flowed from the pierced side of Jesus. Now the death of Jesus tells not only of expiation made, but also of the closing up, under the judgment of God, of our history as of Adam. The life we inherit from the first Adam is only evil in the principle of its will, and in that life we could not live before God. Life, eternal life, flows to us from a heavenly Source, and that Source none other than God's Son. In this life the believer shares even now.

Notice the argument of the apostle in the entire passage. The witness of men we readily receive ; we are obliged to do so about a thousand things. But in human testimony there is a possibility of mistake, even when there is no intention to mislead. With God such a thing is impossible. His witness then is incomparably greater than man's ; and if we give credence to one another's word, how much more ought we to believe God's. Not to believe Him is to make Him a liar. This is strong language, I grant you, but there are the very words in verse 10.

Such is God's testimony to all that believe, such the end for which it has been given. Do you receive this divine testimony ? Do you *know* that eternal life is yours ? If not, why not ?

THE WITNESS:
A FEW MORE WORDS.

The witness of the Spirit is thus seen to be something vastly different from mere happy feelings. To these three things He witnesses :
1. That our sins and iniquities God will remember no more.
2. That we are the children of God.
3. That God hath given unto us eternal life, and this life is in His Son.

Happy are they who in childlike faith have received this three-fold witness.

This brings us to the close of the booklet, written originally for the sake of earnest Cornish folk who longed to " read their title clear " but often found themselves beset by sore misgivings as to their relations with God.

It remains for the present writer to add a very few words.

When the Holy Spirit witnesses with our spirit that we are children of God, His witness undoubtedly takes the form of feelings. He begets within our hearts the feelings, the desires, the affections, that are suitable to the wonderful relationship in which we have been set.

A royal prince may adopt a poor boy. He may bring him into his home circle and give him the place and status of a prince's son. He may clothe him, educate him and treat him in every way in accordance with the relationship into which he has been brought. But he cannot put into him the spirit of the son of a prince, and the boy will feel shy and ill at ease.

Not so with us. God has not only given us the rank and relationship of children, but has put the Spirit of sonship within us, to make us at home in the relationship by producing within us the suitable affections and feelings. In this way we are enabled to enjoy the place into which Divine love has brought us, and to draw near to God with the endearing Name, "Abba, Father" upon our lips. It is not merely that we have assurance. We have holy "boldness" to enter His presence.

THE CHRISTIAN'S BODY.

It is important to observe that it is in our *bodies*, not in our souls, or minds, or consciences that the Holy Spirit is said to dwell. "Know ye not," asks the apostle of the believers at Corinth, "that your *body* is the temple of the Holy Ghost that is in you?" (1 Corinthians vi. 19).

This fact gives great importance to the body, and should make us very careful as to what we read or look at with our eyes, what we say with our tongues, what we do with our hands, what we listen to with our ears, where we go with our feet.

We are not our own. We have been bought with a price, and we belong to Christ. The Holy Spirit is put within us as the Representative of our Owner, and thus our body is His Temple.

This truth involves another. He who indwells us is "the Spirit of Him that raised up Jesus from the dead" (Romans viii. 11). His presence in our bodies is the pledge and proof of what He will do with the bodies in which He dwells. By Him, God will quicken them. The tense is future. The force of "quicken" in the New Testament is "make alive." A quickened body will no longer be subject to decay or death. This great change awaiting our bodies is guaranteed by the fact that the Holy Spirit indwells us.

Through His indwelling our bodies have become the vessels through which God has been glorified and Christ displayed (alas, how feebly!). Therefore God will not let them perish. The same mighty power that has already quickened our souls from a state of spiritual death (Ephesians ii. 5) will touch our bodies. They also shall live the resurrection life, conformed to the likeness of Christ's body of glory (Philippians iii. 21).

Another thing of great interest may be mentioned here. It is noteworthy that the Saviour did things *after His resurrection* by the Holy Spirit. We learn this from Acts i. 2. It suggests that we too shall still have the Spirit dwelling in us in our resurrection state, and that we shall do things by His power. He will be in us the power for worship and holy service in heaven. As a well-known hymn puts it:

> "By *the Spirit, all pervading*,
>   Hosts unnumbered round the Lamb,
> Crowned with light and joy unfading,
>   Hail Him as the great I AM."

How often, in days of sorrow and discouragement we have known "the comfort of the Holy Ghost" (Acts ix. 31). How delightful to think that nothing of what He has been to us down here will be lost to us in heaven!

BLASPHEMING AGAINST THE HOLY SPIRIT.

Blasphemy was always accounted a terrible sin. Under the Mosaic economy no sacrifice could atone for it. The blasphemer was to be stoned to death (Leviticus xxiv. 16).

In these days of grace it is far different. The Lord declared: "All sins shall be forgiven unto the sons of men, and blasphemies wherewith soever they shall blaspheme" (Mark iii. 28). We have a wonderful example of this in the case of Paul the Apostle. In his unregenerate days he was not only a blasphemer himself, but under threat of severe punishment compelled others to blaspheme (Acts xxvi. 11). Yet he was forgiven. As he bears witness: "I . . . was before a blasphemer, and a persecutor, and injurious, but I obtained mercy" (1 Timothy i. 13). Well may he add: "the grace of our Lord was exceeding abundant."

"But ——," and here follows the statement which is regarded by some as being wrapped in unfathomable mystery, and by others as shutting the door of hope finally against them: "But he that shall blaspheme against the Holy Ghost hath never forgiveness" (Mark iii. 29).

This terrible exception to the Saviour's declaration of the possibility of free forgiveness for all has seemed like the knell of doom to some, who conceive the idea that they have committed this sin. They have sinned against light and warning, and have plunged themselves into the depths of despondency, sometimes coupled with a strange, defiant hard-heartedness.

It is impossible to exaggerate the seriousness of a condition like this. It is the result of trifling with the truth of God and with the God of truth, and of sin, unchecked and unjudged in the life.

But for all this, the one who is in this terrible condition is not within a thousand miles of having committed the unpardonable sin ! This awful sin is not what is spoken of as sin against the Holy Ghost, as in Acts v. 3 ; it is more ; it is BLASPHEMY against the Holy Ghost, and is defined in Mark iii. 30 : " They said, He hath an unclean spirit." They actually declared that the Lord of glory was a horrible person, dominated by a vile demon.

If you entertained a thought like this, you would never hear the name of Jesus mentioned without a shudder. You would shun as a pest-house every place where He is worshipped and extolled. You would not allow your children to possess a Bible or listen to a Christian preacher. You would not care even to touch the hand of a believer in Christ. You would regard Christianity as the world's greatest delusion and scourge, a veritable emanation from hell.

THE BACKSLIDER AND THE UNPARDONABLE SIN.

The backslider, however deeply he may have sinned, and however hard his heart and conscience may have become, is not like those wicked scribes who declared that the Holy Ghost was an unclean spirit, and that Jesus was a horrible person, possessed of this unclean spirit. The backslider does not denounce Christ as a fountain of uncleanness ; his quarrel is with himself. He knows that he has only himself to blame, and will acknowledge that Christ is holy and good.

I have sometimes said to people who in their sin and misery imagine that they have committed the unpardonable sin :—

" If I could convince you that salvation is possible, would you desire to be saved ? "

In every instance their reply has been, " Yes, indeed ; how gladly would I seize the chance, if only I had it ! " or words to this effect.

Then I have asked, " By whom would you wish to be saved ? "

" By Christ, of course. He is the only Saviour."

" What ! You would trust for your salvation to a man in the power of an unclean spirit ! Why, surely you would not trust your cat to such a person for half-an-hour, much less your precious soul for all eternity ! "

And in some cases this has been sufficient to let the light in, and to renew hope in the despondent soul. For none of them have ever thought such a horrible thing of the Holy One of God. Yet that is blasphemy against the Holy Ghost ; affirming that He, by whose power the Lord Jesus cast out demons, was Himself an unclean spirit !

Take comfort, poor, despairing backslider. Your sin is grievous, but it is not this sin. The Saviour waits to be gracious ; He will not turn a deaf ear to your penitent cry. Kneel at His feet ; tell Him the sad story of your sin. He will heal your backsliding and help you in your fight against temptation.

A thing which is often erroneously confounded with the unpardonable sin is the " sin unto death " mentioned in 1 John v. 16. This has nothing to do with blasphemy against the Holy Spirit, nor does it come within the range of the subject of this book. It is dealt with in detail in a penny booklet by the writer : " The Unpardonable Sin," to which the reader is referred. It may be obtained from our publisher.

" IF THEY SHALL FALL AWAY."

Does the Epistle to the Hebrews teach that one who has been a partaker of the Holy Spirit may fall away beyond all hope of repentance ? See Chapter vi. 4-6. What can these verses mean ? Is the power of God limited ? Are there some who are beyond even His power to restore ?

Let it be noted that it is not to the ordinary backslider that the writer of this epistle refers. He is speaking of one who, after joining the ranks of Christians, and tasting something of the power and goodness of Christianity, deliberately throws it overboard and returns to Judaism. His argument is that it is of no use to be everlastingly dwelling on the basic truths that lie at the foundation. There is no hope of renewing these apostates by doing so. He will therefore leave them alone and " go on unto perfection." That is, he will proceed to treat of things that belong to Christianity in its completeness, and are in advance of such elementary doctrines as those mentioned in the first two verses of the chapter.

In declaring his inability to move them by anything that he may say or write, he does not deny that it is possible for *God* to renew these renegades to repentance. With Him all things are possible, and to Him none shall turn in vain while the day of grace lasts.

Let us not then, resemble a man to whom an immense fortune is bequeathed and who, while studying the legal documents that assure him that he is the heir, fixes his attention on certain clauses, which he fears may in some way invalidate his title. Confessedly, he does not understand the highly technical language in which these clauses are couched, and a competent lawyer assures him that they refer to another subject altogether. Yet the man worries because some of the terms employed seem to convey a doubt as to his heirship. The lawyer counsels him to read once again the plain statements of the main clause which place beyond all dispute his title to the inheritance, and to rest on these.

Let us follow counsel of this kind, and fix our attention on the many passages of Scripture that assure us that all who trust in the Saviour are truly His. " By Him, all that believe ARE justified from all things " (Acts xiii. 39) ; " Verily, verily, I say unto you, He that believeth on ME HATH everlasting life " (John vi. 47) ; " I give **unto them eternal life, and they** shall never perish, neither shall any man pluck them out of My hand " (John x. 28).

No part of the Word of God can contradict any other part. There are some passages which are admittedly difficult to explain. We shall do well, when reading these, to give heed to a word of wisdom with which Lord Bacon is credited : " Never let what you do not understand rob you of what you do." We may always rest with simple faith upon the plain assurances of the Gospel, and wait upon God for light as to what may be at present beyond our understanding.

" PARTAKERS OF THE HOLY GHOST."

It is conceded that the explanation given in the preceding paragraph does not entirely remove the difficulty of the passage in Hebrews vi. Can " partakers of the Holy Ghost " fall away so hopelessly ? Does not the term imply true conversion on the part of those made partakers of the Holy Spirit ?

Not necessarily. As we have remarked elsewhere, Balaam, though a wicked man, had the Spirit of God come upon him (Numbers xxiv. 2) So had Saul, who afterwards became king, and developed into a thoroughly bad man (1 Samuel x. 10). Both these evil men were able to prophesy because of this. This suggests that there may be such a thing as being used by the Spirit of God without being sealed and indwelt by Him; having Him professionally, as it were.

In the Parable of the Ten Virgins, when the foolish ones awoke they exclaimed, " Our lamps are *going out* " (R.V., Matthew xxv. 8). That is, their lamps had oil sufficient to keep them alight the whole time that they were asleep, but they had none *in their vessels with their lamps*. It is generally agreed that the oil is an emblem here, as elsewhere, of the Holy Spirit, and that the lamps stand for profession. The lesson seems to be that it is possible to have the Holy Spirit's work and blessing in connection with our profession and our service, while not possessing Him in reality. In such a case, as with the foolish virgins, there is no vital link with Christ. He will say " I know you not," for " if any man *have* not the Spirit of Christ, he is none of His " (Romans viii. 9).

One may be a " servant," and do useful things as Judas did, and as hundreds more have done, and yet eventually share the fate of those who never made any profession (Luke xii. 46). To persuade people who are in the ranks of Christian profession, and are thus " partakers " or " companions " of the Holy Spirit in the same outward way that Judas was a companion of Christ, that they will get to heaven after a period of future punishment is an evil work. Persons who are not *indwelt* by the Holy Spirit are no real Christians at all.

They may " believe," but their believing is but transient. In the language of Christ Himself, they "*for a while believe*" and then fall away (Luke viii. 13).

The geniune believer may backslide, but he does not apostatize. Those described in Hebrews vi. 4, 5 are not true believers. The five things said of them may be true of mere professors. And if there is such a thing as sharing in the power of the Holy Spirit *officially*, it behoves us all the more to make sure that we have the vital link with Christ, and are sealed as belonging to Him.

ACCESS BY ONE SPIRIT.

These words occur in one of the few verses that mention every One of the three Persons of the Godhead : Ephesians ii. 18. Will the reader turn to it, consider it carefully, then try to answer this question : Why is the Holy Spirit mentioned ? Would not the verse have been complete if it were simply " For through Him we both have access unto the Father " ?

The " we both " is, of course, converted Jew and converted Gentile. Both have been reconciled to God in one body by the Cross (verse 16) and through Him who suffered there both have the privilege of drawing nigh to the Father. It not this enough ? Why is the Holy Spirit brought in ?

The answer is to be found in the full meaning of the word " access." It means more than an open door and the right of entrance. Beside this, it means *going through it*. By the atoning sacrifice of Christ the door is opened wide. There are folks who are continually praising God for this. But they seem to have no desire to pass through the open door and explore the great things of the Father.

This is where the work of the Holy Spirit comes in. It is Christ whom by the shedding of His blood, has made access to the Father possible. It is the Holy Spirit who leads us to avail ourselves of this possibility. Christ has thrown the door wide open ; the Holy Spirit takes us by the hand, as it were, and conducts us through it.

Let us pull ourselves up sometimes with a little wholesome self-examination. We need not ask ourselves how often we have thanked God that the door is open, and that nothing remains to bar us from His presence. But let us ask ourselves : How long do I spend each day in the place to which that open door leads ? How often do I *use* the open door ? What do I know of the vast treasures of love and of knowledge on the other side of it ?

Queen Esther dared not enter the presence of her own husband. When at last she bravely decided to do so, she realised that she carried her life in her hand. " If I perish, I perish ! " she said. We have no such fear in drawing nigh to God, for He is our Father. And by the Holy Spirit who indwells us we are able to enjoy His love, and become conversant with all that He has revealed of His thoughts.

AN HABITATION OF GOD THROUGH THE SPIRIT.

Of some men we say, " Oh, he lives in his garden." We mean that Mr. A.'s garden is his chief interest. He spends all his leisure hours therein.

Another man " lives in his books." He is a bookworm and is never happier than when he sits in front of his bookshelves with nobody to disturb him.

Yet another "lives in his business." Not the love of money, but the love of getting it, dominates him. He dreams of it at night, and even on Sunday he is making his plans for Monday. He is never so miserable as when he is " enjoying " an enforced holiday.

Of other men it can be said : " he lives in God " (1 John iv. 16). God is his chief interest. To Him his soul turns in its leisure moments. He has found the very home of his heart in God. He " dwelleth in God."

This will help us a little to understand the tremendous import of the statement in Ephesians ii. 22, from which the seven words at the head of this paragraph are quoted. **It is the opposite of what we learned from 1 John.** The truth here is that God dwells in us. We (even we Gentiles) are built together that God might live in us ; that He might find the home of His great, strong affections in us ; that we might be a dwelling place for Him.

When time has ceased to be, and we find ourselves in eternity, God will dwell with men and bless them for ever with His unveiled presence. But it is by means of His tabernacle that He does this (Revelation xxi. 3). Dwelling *in* His tabernacle, He dwells *with* men. May we not identify the " habitation " of to-day with the " tabernacle " of to-morrow ? Now, God dwells in His redeemed ones, built together as one, by the Spirit. By the Spirit He has taken possession of His habitation and does in it what pleases Him, just as we order things in our homes for our own pleasure. The more we think of this, the more amazed we shall be.

STRENGTHENED WITH MIGHT BY HIS SPIRIT.

Probably there is no reader of these pages who does not feel his own spiritual weakness, and who would not readily admit his need of being " strengthened with might by His Spirit in the inner man " (Ephesians iii. 16).

If, however, the question were asked, *Why* do you desire this ? what a variety of answers would be given ! Some would say they need to be strengthened that they might have a larger measure of spiritual vigour for service. Others would say that they need to be strengthened in order that they might endure hardness and trial and, if needs be, suffer for Christ's sake.

This is very good. But what Paul prayed for was that those to whom he wrote might be strengthened, not only that they might have Christ dwelling in their hearts by faith, but that they might *comprehend* and *know*.

The thoughts of God are wonderful, and infinite in number. We cannot classify them ; they rush together, overlap and coalesce. We cannot reckon them up in order when we are before God in prayer and thanksgiving (Psalm xl. 5). The sum of them is great indeed (Psalm cxxxix. 17) ; but all are summed up in Christ. The revelation of all God's thoughts is overpowering. We cannot comprehend them. They stagger and confound us.

Then, strengthened with might by His Spirit, we are made at home in the midst of them. After all, it is a question of the heart, and Christ, the Sum and Substance of the breadth, length, depth and height of God's thoughts and purposes, dwells there. Thus we are made, in some measure, to understand them, and to know the love of Christ, a knowledge that is better worth having than the knowledge of anything else.

When great things were revealed to Daniel in vision " there remained no strength " in him (Daniel x. 8). Words that he heard produced the same effect (verse 17). Then a glorious one, who had spoken to him, touched him and strengthened him (verse 18). The result of this strengthening was that Daniel was prepared to listen to further unfoldings. He said : " Let my lord speak, for thou hast strengthened me " (verse 19).

Even so is it, when we are strengthened by God's Spirit in the inner man.

THE FRUIT OF THE SPIRIT.

The fruits of righteousness, we read, are by Jesus Christ. He is their source ; they were seen to perfection in Him when He was here. But it is the Holy Spirit's work to reproduce the character of Christ in us. The apostle prays that the Christians at Philippi may be filled with these " fruits of righteousness " (Philippians i. 9-11) ; in other words that what marked Christ might now mark them.

The fruit of the Spirit, that is, the result of His indwelling and of His gracious work in us, is described in Galatians v. 22, 23. The works of the flesh, ennumerated in the preceding verses, are the very opposite. In the case of the Galatians, Law, appealing to the flesh on the line of restraint and improvement, only awakened its lust. These horrible works were the result. Grace, making no demand, but working to produce, could point to the delightful " fruit of the Spirit " as the outcome.

It is not that we are to be unduly occupied with the work of the Spirit within. We are to set our affection, our mind, on things above, where Christ is. As we look up to Him, and find in Him the Object of our love, we are empowered to *put off* the ugly works of the flesh and *put on* the lovely character of Christ (Colossians iii. 2, 8, 12).

The Spirit of God works to reproduce in us the likeness of the One with whom we are occupied. It is not a question so much of trusting Him as studying Him ; it is a matter of love rather than of faith. Loving Him, we come to resemble Him, and thus the Spirit produces in our lives love, joy, peace, long-suffering, gentleness, goodness, faith, meekness, self-control.

God looks down upon such lives and says, as it were : " There is something of Christ ; it is too precious to be lost ; I will see that it is all gathered up to find its place eventually in glory." Thus Christ in us, reproduced by the Spirit, becomes the pledge of glory by-and-by. Is not this the meaning of Colossians i. 27 : " Christ in you, the hope of glory " ?

THE SPIRIT OF LIFE IN CHRIST JESUS.

How strong is the law, or principle, of sin and death ! Sin is followed by spiritual death (Romans vi. 11). The downward pull of these awful things is terriffic. Well may the wretched man of Romans vii. 24 exclaim, " Who shall deliver me from the body of this death ? "

Is there no deliverance ? Are we, as long as we are on earth, to be hopelessly delivered over to this principle, the principle of sin and death ? We know that we shall be set free when we leave this world, but is there no such thing as *present* emancipation ?

Listen to the triumphant paean of Romans viii. 2 : " *free* from the law of sin and death ! " Something had made Paul free ! What was it ?

It was another principle, one of superior power. You watch an aeroplane rise from the ground and ask,

"What frees it from the law of gravitation that always pulls it downward?" Someone replies: "The law of aviation has made it free from the law of gravitation"

Read the verse in Romans viii. in the light of this illustration. Think first of Christ Jesus. This is His title as the risen, glorious Man in heaven. "He liveth unto God" (Romans vi. 10). Try to think of His life up there, its joys, its activities, its pursuits, the very atmosphere in which it is lived: eternal love. Now think of *the Spirit of that life*. He is the One Who, in real power, brings to us here all that that life in heaven means. It attracts and absorbs us. Our souls expand in it. We breathe, as it were, the atmosphere of that heavenly life. Its joys, its pursuits, are ours. The Spirit makes them real to us.

What now of the law, the principle, of sin and death? In the way we have described we have been emancipated from it. A superior principle has delivered us from its downward pull. This superior principle is, that the Spirit who dwells in us is the Spirit of that wonderful life which we ourselves shall actually live in heaven by-and-by, the life which Christ, our Head and Representative, already lives. The Spirit enables us to enter, in some measure at least, into that life even now. And in the measure in which this is true, He has set us, practically and experimentally, free from the law of sin and death.

THE SPIRIT OF SONSHIP.

There is a great difference between the teaching of Romans viii. and a section of the Epistle to the Galatians that apparently deals with the same subject. In Romans we read of "the Spirit of sonship" (for this is the real meaning of the Spirit of adoption, viii. 15); while in Galatians iv. 6 we read of "the Spirit of His Son." Both passages deal with our relationship to God as His sons.

The difference is this: Romans contrasts the present with the glorious future; Galatians contrasts the present with the superseded past.

To speak first of Romans. As to our bodies, we are still part of a groaning creation. But we have been set in the relationship to God of sons. This implies glory and manifestation, which are not yet ours. For these we wait. Indeed the whole creation awaits our manifestation (verse 19). In the glorious future we shall receive the rank and glory that belong to the relationship. At present we are the sons of God travelling *incognito* through a world which owns another as its god and prince. But we have already received *the Spirit of sonship* (verse 15), so that the relationship is already known, and we enjoy holy intimacy with God our Father.

In Galatians the Apostle is speaking of those that had been Jews. Till Christ came, they were in the position of minors, like wards put under guardians and trustees. They had not the status of sons, nor could they address God as "Father." When Christ came, He redeemed those that were in bondage under the Law, and revealed God as Father. Those who had been but minors emerged thus into full age, as it were. They received sonship in the sense that they were no longer "shut up" and "under tutors and governors," but were emancipated into the status of sons.

Moreover, "the Spirit of His Son" came to dwell in them, not only that the feelings and affections suitable to sons might be found in them (as in Romans), but that the very feelings and affections of the Beloved One Himself might well up within them.

Wonderful indeed ! And it is as true of us as of those who lived long ago !

THE CROSS AND THE SPIRIT.

What a lot we find about the Holy Spirit in the second chapter of 1 Corinthians ! We cannot recall any chapter in the New Testament that has so much to say about Him, except Romans viii. What is the reason ?

Various evils had found their way into the church at Corinth, and the Christians seemed little concerned thereby. In connection with a case of the grossest immorality they were " puffed up " (v. 2) ; they were probably proud of their tolerance. Perhaps they called it " charity," though it was nothing but sinful laxity.

As a corrective of all this the Apostle, in chapters i. and ii. has much to say about the cross, and the crucifixion. See Chapter i. 13, 17, 18, 23 ; Chapter ii. 2, 8. The cross closes the door against sin, the flesh, and the world. It is not only that the Saviour died thereon for our salvation, but that it stands as an impassable barrier between us and the world, between us and all that to which Christ died. Behind that closed door are our sins, our judgment, and our own evil selves.

But there is an open door, as well as a closed one, and in this connection the Holy Spirit is brought in. It is He who leads us through that open door into the wonderful things of God.

Notice seven remarkable things affirmed concerning the Holy Spirit in Chapter ii.

1. He knows the things of God, just as the human spirit knows the things of a man (verse 11).

2. The things of the Spirit of God are not receivable by the natural man. Can a goat receive lessons in chemistry ? Is not all the scientific apparatus foolishness to it ? Even so, the things of the Spirit are foolishness to the natural man (verse 14).

3. The Spirit which we have received is not the spirit of the world but the Spirit of God (verse 12). We cannot therefore be at home in the world ; we are at home in God's things.

4. He searches (on our behalf) the deep things of God (verse 10).

5. God has revealed to us by His Spirit the things that He has in view for us (verse 10).

6. The Holy Spirit gives words for the communication of the things of God (verse 13).

7. The Holy Spirit clothes with power these words that He gives (verse 4), so that the message goes forth " in demonstration of the Spirit and of power."

God grant we may learn the secret of the closed door and the open door !

THE SPIRIT'S DAY.

It is sometimes said, often, we fear, with the object of discouraging large expectations, that we live in " a day of small things." Is this true ?

The words are a quotation from Zechariah iv. 10. The day to which they refer was indeed a day of small things. The new temple had just been erected. It was a small structure. When the glory of the temple built

THE HOLY SPIRIT Here Today 145

by Solomon was remembered, the new one was "in comparision of it as nothing" (Haggai ii. 3).

Littleness was characteristic of what we may call Israel's day. The nation commenced its existence as "the fewest of all people" (Deut. vii. 7). Later on, when the fighting forces of the ten tribes were at full strength ("the children of Israel were numbered and *were all present*"), they were but as "two little flocks of kids" beside the Syrians (1 Kings xx. 27). When the southern kingdom (Judah) became leavened with vice, it was but " a very small remnant" that remained (Isaiah i. 9). In the days of the exile, God graciously raised the spirits of some (Ezra i. 5); but the revival was very limited in scope. Ezra spoke of it as "a little reviving" (chapter ix. 8). The majority preferred to remain in the lands of the Gentiles, as the book of Esther shows. God did not forget His exiled people. But He promised them no great things, but said He would be as "a little sanctuary" to them in those distant countries.

What a difference the coming into the world of the Son of God made! What *great* things He introduced! And these great things became characteristic of this, the day of the Holy Spirit, the day in which our lot is cast. It may be a day of small men, but (unlike Zechariah's day) it is a day of great *things*. This appears in the Acts of the Apostles.

In the Old Testament we keep company with kings, and with prophets who were addressed as "my lord Moses," "my lord Elijah." In the New Testament we move along with fishermen and the like. But more especially we find ourselves in the presence of the greatest of all: the Holy Spirit.

To what great things is He the key!

Instead of being a day of small things this, the Holy Spirit's day, is the day of :—

(1) A GREAT LIGHT, Acts xxii. 6. A light shines for us, not only transcending in brightness all that ever shone for Israel, but surpassing any that will shine in the future. At the advent of Christ, when He comes to establish His Kingdom, He will shine forth as the Sun (Malachi iv. 2). But the light that shines for us is a light *above* the brightness of the sun (Acts xxvi. 13). It is a light that reveals not only the very nature of God, but the purposes of His eternal love ; a light that discloses the amazing fact that tried and persecuted saints on earth are part of Christ Himself, for He speaks of them as " Me."

MORE GREAT THINGS.

Other great things that characterise the present day, in contrast with the " small things " which pertained to the day of Zechariah, are as follows :—

(2) A GREAT SHEET, Acts x. 11. This sets forth the world-wide scope of the grace of God to-day. In former times the river of God's mercy was continually overflowing its banks. It overflowed to Rahab the Canaanite, Ruth the Moabitess, Naaman the Syrian, and a whole city full of Ninevites. But there are no banks for it to overflow in this day. It is like a shoreless ocean, flowing free to all mankind, and bringing those whom it reaches to better blessing than Israel ever knew.

(3) A GREAT MULTITUDE, Acts xiv. 1. It is not only that there is grace for all, but that grace has been effectual.

Three thousand were gathered in by means of Peter's memorable discourse on the day of Pentecost. But on how many days since has this number been surpassed ? Is it not probable that last Sunday, for instance, more than 3,000, all the world over, were added to the Lord ? Christians, the disciples of Christ, if only they could be viewed all together, would be seen to be a great multitude indeed !

(4) GREAT POWER, Acts iv. 33. This is characteristic of this, the Spirit's day. " God hath not given us the Spirit of fear ; but *of power* " (2 Timothy i. 7). An electric car in a city is driven by the power that reaches it from overhead wires or some other means. The power that drives that car is the power that drives *all* the cars of that system. So, the power that is behind the whole testimony of God on earth is the power behind each individual Christian, the power of the Holy Spirit.

(5) GREAT GRACE, Acts iv. 33. The day in which we live is rightly called the day of grace. The grace is commensurate with the power. Power without grace would be misused. The yachts that have the biggest masts and carry the heaviest weight of canvas have the deepest keels, to keep them from heeling over. The more the power of the Holy Spirit is manifested in connection with our testimony, our walk, and our service, the more we shall need a supply of that great grace from God's inexhaustible storehouse. It is " manifold " grace (1 Peter iv. 10), many-sided and applicable in a multitude of ways. And the One from Whom it comes is the God of *all* grace (1 Peter v. 10). There is assuredly no lack with Him.

THE HEIRESS AND THE KEY.

At a wedding in New York the bride, daughter of a millionaire, received from her father the present of a latch-key. There was a stir among the guests and several expressed surprise. But the bride smiled, and took possession of the key. She knew what it meant. The actual present was a substantial mansion, beautifully furnished. The key was a token that the house was hers. It was also the means by which she could enter into possession of the gift.

In like manner the Holy Spirit is the key to the great things of God. The fact that He indwells us is the pledge that all is ours, and He Himself is the power by which we enter experimentally into the possession and enjoyment thereof. The Scriptures bear witness to the fact that all these blessings are ours. By faith we receive their testimony and are assured of our possessions. But we are not speaking now of assurance, but of enjoyed possession.

All this puts us in a definite position with regard to the world. We belong to it no longer, and it looks upon us with no favourable eye. The outcome, from the beginning, has been another of the *great* things that are characteristic of the present day. We have enumerated five. There are two other, mentioned in the acts.

(6) GREAT PERSECUTION, Acts viii. 1. It is not that persecution did not exist before. Elijah was persecuted by Jezebel; Jeremiah was flung into a pit. But the persecution meted out to *Christians* far surpasses all that went before. Hundreds of thousands were brutally done to death in the days of Pagan Rome. And millions of true-hearted saints have been tortured and butchered by the wearers of mitre and cowl. Then think of China,

of Madagascar, of Armenia, of Russia, of Spain. Even in our day persecution has reached huge proportions.

(7) GREAT JOY, Acts viii. 3 and xv. 3. What joy can compare with the joy that Christians have, even amid the fires of fierce persecution ? It is not merely the joy of deliverance, such as the people of Israel knew on the eastern bank of the Red Sea, but the joy of souls sharing the love of God, and knowing the Risen Christ as the the One to whom they belong.

Then let us praise God that our lot is cast, not in " a day of small things " but in a day of things transcendently great, the day of the Holy Spirit.

THE HOLY SPIRIT AND THE WORLD.

No worldling can receive the Holy Spirit. He may pray for this great gift, but God never bestows His Spirit upon any save those who believe in Christ for salvation. The words are very clear : " Whom the world cannot receive " (John xiv. 17).

The world did not receive Christ, but He was in it, testified to it, and sought to save men out of it. In like manner the Holy Spirit, though not received by the world, is here. And His presence carries with it certain implications.

(1) He reproves, or convicts, the world of sin, because it has not believed on Christ (John xvi. 8, 9). This passage does not refer to the work of the Spirit in producing conviction of sin in the souls of sinners. He does that. But the truth of this passage is that the Holy Spirit's coming is a proof of the departure of Christ from the world in consequence of His having been rejected.

(2) He reproves, or convicts, the world of righteousness; that is, in connection with righteousness. Christ was treated with shameful unrighteousness in the world; but, as it was written in Psalm xxiv. 5: "He shall receive . . . righteousness from the God of His salvation," He has received righteous treatment in heaven, and has been set in the place that is His by right. The Holy Spirit's presence here is a demonstration of this.

(3) He reproves, or convicts, the world of judgment, in that the prince of this world (Satan) has been dispossessed. Christ is Heir of all things, the true Proprietor of this earth. The Holy Spirit, being here on behalf of Christ, proves by His very presence that the world's prince has been judged, and they who have submitted to be ruled by him must share his judgment.

All this is developed and enlarged on in the Book of Revelation. There the voice of the Spirit is heard addressing the churches first, and then testifying not so much *to as against* this Christ-rejecting world.

THE HOLY SPIRIT AND HYMNS.

The hymnology of the Holy Spirit in the English language (and, as far as I know, in every other language) is exceedingly poor. There are hymns which consist of prayers *for* the coming of the Spirit, a thing, as we have shown, most unsuitable for these days of His residence and presence here.

Then there are hymns addressed *to* the Holy Spirit, in defiance of the manifest fact that prayers and praises are never addressed to Him in Scripture. Christians, if they sing these hymns, do so in ignorance, or else they do violence to their intelligence.

The writer, some years ago, got together a few Scriptural hymns that might be intelligently sung at meetings where the Person and Work of the Holy Spirit were the subject of the discourse. Some were written for the purpose, and all were printed as a separate hymn sheet, published by the Central Bible Truth Depot, London.

Edward Whyte, an Edinburgh dentist (now " absent from the body, present with the Lord ") contributed the following, which may be sung to the same tune as " Our blest Redeemer, ere He breathed ":

1 O GOD, how glorious is Thy grace,
    Rich mercy all divine ;
  We live in love before Thy face,
    By blood made Thine.

2 Exceeding great Thy power revealed
    In us, once slaves of sin ;
  Now with Thy Holy Spirit sealed,
    He dwells within.

3 To us He is the Earnest true
    Of riches yet in store ;
  The wealth of heaven He brings to view
    Still more and more.

4 Oh, heavenly gift from Christ on high !
    Oh, gift of priceless worth,
  To bring to us these glories nigh,
    While still on earth !

5 Borne by His power, our souls in **strength**
    Would tread that realm above :
  Its height and depth, its breadth and **length,**
    And know Christ's love.

6 Our Father God, Thy children's praise
    Is music to Thine ear ;
  The Spirit prompts the song we raise,
    And brings us near.

7 And while the desert way we roam,
    We'll know the tender care
  Of Him Who leads us safely home :
    The COMFORTER.

David Scougall, a business man, also of Edinburgh, sent a hymn of eight verses :

1 THERE is in every Christian's breast
    A secret spring of heavenly joy ;
  'Tis by no other heart possessed,
    And nothing can that spring alloy.

2 A heavenly Guest therein abides,
    Sent by the Father from above,
  Who knows the vast exhaustless tides
    And treasures of the Father's love.

3 He loves these treasures to impart
    To all who are redeemed by blood,
  And in each longing pilgrim's heart
    To shed the love of God abroad.

4 He loves to dry the Christian's tears
    And all his woes and fears dispel ;
  And aye the drooping heart He cheers
    With glories He delights to tell :

5 The glories of the heavenly land
    And of the risen Saviour there,
  In Whom we live, in Whom we stand,
    Who shall with us those glories share.

6 But over misspent hours He grieves,
    And ponders still the steps we take ;
Yet, ever faithful, never leaves
    Those who are loved for Jesus' sake.

7 He ever, like a trusty Guide,
    Conducts us on our homeward way,
Which leads to where true joys abide,
    And guards our footsteps lest we stray.

8 Blest Father, we unite our praise
    For this good Gift Thy love has given ;
Henceforward let our words and ways
    Speak less of earth and more of heaven.

A hymn that has appeared in several hymn books is a composite one, the first two verses being by Geo. Cutting, the author of " Safety, Certainty and Enjoyment," the remaining two by a well-known evangelist, Alfred Mace.

1 O GRACIOUS Saviour, Thou hast given
    My trembling soul to know
That, trusting in Thy precious blood,
    I'm washed as white as snow.

2 Since Thou hast borne sin's heavy load,
    My guilty fear is o'er ;
Made Thine, by virtue of Thy blood,
    I'm sealed for evermore.

3 What wait I for, most blessed Lord,
    Except Thy face to see ?
If such the Earnest Thou hast given,
    What must Thy presence be ?

4 To hear Thy voice, to see Thy face,
   And grieve Thy heart no more,
But drink the fulness of Thy grace,
   Thy love for evermore.

Another hymn is, we believe, by Mr. W. J. Hocking, the Editor of an expository magazine :

1 O GRACIOUS God, our Father,
   We thank Thee for Thy Word,
To all our hearts so precious
   That speaks of Christ the Lord ;
We thank Thee for Thy Spirit
   That moved those men of old,
Who in the holy record
   Thy truth and love unfold.

2 For the same One we bless Thee,
   The Earnest and the Seal,
Who doth to Thine own children
   Thy mind and will reveal ;
As none but He who knows it
   The truth could e'er impart,
So none but those He teacheth
   Receive it in the heart.

3 Oh, may we then, blest Father,
   Thy gracious Word believe,
That we may by the Spirit
   The truth in love receive :
For we would thus be girded
   To serve our faithful Lord,
And in this day of conflict,
   Cleave to His Name and Word.

The hymn that follows was written partly, if not wholly, by Arthur Cutting, a younger brother of George Cutting, well known as an evangelist :

1 PARDONED and sealed, through Jesus' precious blood,
    In God's own changeless love we're fully blessed ;
  His Spirit, witnessing we're sons of God,
    Is now the Earnest of eternal rest.

2 Grant us, O God, that He may thus reveal
    The length, breadth, depth and height, and Jesus' love,
  And on our souls its holy impress seal,
    Till we its fulness know with Him above.

3 May He, our Guide into all truth divine,
    Give rich, increasing knowledge of Thy Word,
  And show the glories that in Jesus shine,
    That we may love Him more, our precious Lord.

4 May He, as Intercessor, teach us how
    To pray according to Thy holy will ;
  Cause us with deep and strong desire to glow,
    And our whole soul with earnest longing fill.

5 And may His comforts cheer us when distressed,
    And gently soothe our sorrow, calm our grief,
  Helping to find, upon our Saviour's breast,
    In every hour of trial, sure relief.

There is another good hymn by Arthur Cutting:

1 O GOD, our hearts are lifted
    To Thee in grateful praise;
Responsive to Thy Spirit,
    A joyful song we raise;
For He Thy gracious purpose
    In Christ to us has shown,
That now as sons before Thee
    His favour is our own.

2 In nature's darkness shrouded,
    And dead in sins we lay
Until Thy Holy Spirit
    Transformed our night to day;
Awakened needs within us,
    Begetting us anew,
And by love's strong compelling,
    Our souls to Jesus drew.

3 We trusted Him as Saviour,
    When rest and peace we sought;
Thou graciously hast sealed us,
    As those His blood has bought;
Thy Spirit ne'er will leave us,
    For He is pledged to stay
As Earnest of our portion,
    Until redemption's day.

4 Oh, may Thy Holy Spirit,
    Blest Unction from on high,
With all His rich infilling,
    Lead us to glorify
The risen Christ, our Saviour,
    By loyal witness true,
Constraining us to serve Him,
    In all we say and do.

The next hymn is a composite one, five verses being by the writer of this book, the remaining two by Arthur Cutting :

> 1 WE praise Thee for Thy Spirit, Lord,
>   The blessed Holy Ghost,
>   The promised Comforter from heaven
>   Who came at Pentecost.
>
> 2 We praise Thee for His wondrous grace
>   That broke our darkness through,
>   And wrought within us by Thy Word
>   A birth divinely new.
>
> 3 We praise Thee that He is the Seal
>   Whereby we're marked as Thine
>   Until redemption's day shall dawn
>   And we in glory shine.
>
> 4 We praise Thee for the Earnest given
>   Of blessings yet in store,
>   The great inheritance which we
>   Shall share for evermore.
>
> 5 We praise Thee that the Unction sent
>   Abides in us for aye,
>   To be our Teacher, Guide and Strength
>   Along life's upward way.
>
> 6 We praise Thee for those ties divine
>   That bind Thy saints to Thee
>   As members of Thy body one,
>   The Spirit's unity.
>
> 7 We praise Thee for the work which He
>   Hath in our souls begun,
>   To form in us a transcript here
>   Of God's beloved Son.

A hymn, which, if we mistake not, is an adaptation of one already existing, we know not by whom, is the following :

1 O GOD, we thank Thee for Thy Holy Spirit,
    Dwelling within, the Comforter divine ;
May He our lives make fruitful for Thy glory,
    Proving to all that we by grace are Thine.

2 May we no hindrance offer to His working,
    Nor may we grieve Him as He seeks to fill
Our hearts with Christ, that we may be more like Him,
    Ever more subject to Thy holy will.

3 May He His goodly fruit produce within us,
    LOVE, deep and full, to God and all mankind;
JOY in the Lord, 'mid every earthly sorrow ;
    PEACE, calm and sweet, that guardeth heart and mind.

4 LONGSUFFERING, 'mid earth's fiercest provocations ;
    GENTLENESS, when enduring cruel wrong ;
GOODNESS, that we our foes may kindly succour;
    FAITHFULNESS, since we now to Christ belong.

5 MEEKNESS, combined with fixed and stedfast purpose ;
    And SELF-CONTROL, through His controlling might ;
Then, as we seek to serve our Lord and Master,
    We would do all as in His holy sight.

Another useful hymn has been made out of fragments of two old ones, with new material added :—

> 1 SOON the saints, in glory singing,
>   Will with joy exalt the Lamb ;
>   All in heaven, their tribute bringing,
>   Loud His glorious worth proclaim ;
>   Every voice, with gladness ringing,
>   Raising high the Saviour's name.
>
> 2 Now to us the Earnest's given,
>   We by grace to Christ belong ;
>   All our many sins forgiven,
>   Theme of praise for every tongue !
>   Sing we now, as soon in heaven,
>   Strains of everlasting song.
>
> 3 God Himself, His love revealing,
>   Calls us sons, and hath bestowed
>   His great gift, the Spirit, sealing
>   Those redeemed to Him by blood ;
>   We, His gracious gift receiving,
>   " Abba, Father " cry aloud.
>
> 4 This high honour we inherit,
>   And, till Jesus comes, we pray
>   That His matchless love and merit
>   Fill our hearts both night and day,
>   And the unction of His Spirit
>   All our thoughts and actions sway.
>
> 5 Ere the day of Christ's appearing,
>   Spirit-taught, His heavenly Bride
>   Views with joy His advent nearing,
>   Longs to see Him glorified ;
>   All His deepest joys then sharing,
>   Love for ever satisfied.

There are other hymns on the hymn-sheet, which are found in other collections. Most or all of those given here have been included in an admirable book compiled by W. H. Knox, of Seven Kings, one of the best hymn-books for worship, the breaking of bread, and general use. But there is a great dearth of hymns that convey truth, and not error, on the subject of the Holy Spirit. Perhaps some of our readers, gifted with the ability to write poetry, may be led to do something in this line.

THE UNCTION.

It is somewhat of a mystery why our translators should have given us two words in 1 John ii, " unction " in verse 20 and " anointing " in verse 27 for the original " chrisma." But the reference in each verse is, of course, to the Holy Spirit, with whom God has anointed us (2 Corinthians i. 21).

In ancient days a king was anointed prior to his coronation. See 1 Sam. x. 1 and xvi. 13, where we read of the anointing first of Saul, then of David. Where the oil was poured, the crown would be placed later on.

But the anointing with oil was not only a pledge of future coronation. The one who was anointed was presumed, from that day, to be a kingly man, and to have kingly feelings ; to conduct himself in a kingly way.

With something similar in view we have been anointed, not with oil, but with the Holy Spirit. To us a kingly law is given (James ii. 8) ; none but a kingly race can fulfil it. Our priesthood is a kingly one (1 Peter ii. 9) ; as such we are to exhibit the character of God. Our testimony is to shew forth His praises.

But in 1 John ii a further thought is connected with the Unction, namely *power of discernment*. Already " many antichrists " were doing their sinister work ; evil men were seducing the saints. Their words were plausible, their sophistries not easy to see through. To whom should the perplexed believers betake themselves ? Whose counsel should they seek ?

The apostle answers these questions by reminding them that they had an Unction from the Holy One, and thus knew all things (1 John ii. 20). This does not mean, of course, that they were perfect in knowledge, but that all that they needed in order to know right from wrong, truth from error, was this Anointing from on high.

In verse 27 of the same chapter the apostle goes further. " Ye need not that any man teach you," he says. They needed no one to say " This is right and true " and " That is erroneous and wrong " for the Holy Spirit, abiding in them as the Anointing, was sufficient to give them all needed knowledge as to these things. He would give them powers of discernment that they could gain from no human source.

THE WINNING SIDE.

It is the day of the great annual University boat race in England. The streets of every town are full of men, women and even children wearing blue rosettes. Dark blue is the Oxford colour ; light blue that of Cambridge. By and by the news comes through : Cambridge has won. Note the air of exultation on the part of the wearers of the light blue ! They walk with a more elastic step. They make the streets resonant with their shouts.

Again, a war is in progress. News reaches one of the belligerent nations that its fighting forces have won a great victory. Flags are hoisted; the bells begin to ring out their merry chimes; men shake each other by the hand. Everywhere there is rejoicing. There is an air of triumph.

Something of this kind, only with two important differences, seems to be indicated by the expression: "The Spirit of glory and of God resteth upon you" (1 Peter iv. 14). Please spell the word Spirit with a capital S, for the reference is undoubtedly to the Holy Spirit.

The first difference of which I have made mention is this. *It is not merely that* WE *wear the mien of triumph, but One who dwells within us does.* It is the Holy Spirit Himself who exults in the victory. If we also exult it is because He, as the Spirit of glory, rests upon us. He begets within us the rejoicing, and produces in us the marks of those who are the sharers of a resounding triumph.

Secondly, the Spirit of glory thus rests upon us *before the final victory is achieved*. We are still partakers of Christ's sufferings, still exposed to reproach for His Names' sake. But all the time we know we are on the winning side, and deport ourselves accordingly. The Spirit of glory, resting upon us, gives us the emotions of those who celebrate the triumph of the side that they have espoused in a conflict. We have the assurance that He who bruised Satan under the feet of Christ at Calvary will shortly bruise him under *our feet* (Romans xvi. 20). We joyfully anticipate the glorious result of this. With music in our souls, and melodies of praise upon our lip we exult in the certainty of the glory that will ensue.

Even if flung into prison, we can sing to God with gladness of heart (Acts xvi. 25). We can sing at funerals, in the very face of death. For the Spirit of glory already rests upon us. We pursue the ways of life as those who are heirs of glory and of God.

WORSHIPPING BY THE SPIRIT.

It is a pity that our ordinary Bibles have the word " Spirit " in Philippians iii. 3 spelt with a small " s." For beyond a doubt Paul is speaking of the Holy Spirit. He links three things together : (1) worshipping God in, or by, the Spirit, (2) rejoicing in Christ Jesus, and (3) having no confidence in the flesh.

There can be no acceptable worship of God where any of these things is lacking. To be rejoicing in Christ is most essential. Without this worship degenerates into mere thanksgiving. If a friend does a kind action for me I thank him, but I do not worship him. So worship transcends thanking God for His mercies. The highest form of worship is to speak to God about the excellencies of His beloved Son. We can only do this when we are rejoicing in Him.

A lady who has one son, a sailor away in the far east, invites me to tea. She gives me a dainty and delicious repast. I have an hour to remain for conversation afterwards. Which will please my kind hostess more : for me to keep thanking her over and over again for her lovely cake and home-made jam, or to talk with her about her son, whom she dearly loves ? Only one answer is possible. Let us bear it in mind if ever we are tempted to think that we are worshipping God when we are only thanking Him for His bountiful gifts.

At the same time, if the Holy Spirit is to have His way with us, there must be the disallowance of the flesh. The flesh, that evil principle within us with which we were born into the world, is neither removed nor improved at our conversion. It will, if permitted, intrude into the holiest things. We may think we can make use of it in the service of God. It may present itself under the guise of " great earnestness " or " great simplicity." It may take the form of self-assertion and self-confidence. But if our worship is to be truly by the Holy Spirit, the flesh (which is only another way of spelling " self ") must be recognised and refused ; it must be judged as something that is hateful to God.

Then, with the evil, unsuitable material judged and refused, and with Christ as the One in whom our souls have found their delight, we may draw near to God in His Name. And the Holy Spirit will lead us into the realm of God's wonderful things, where Christ is all in all, and this will be our material for worship.

We must remember the teaching of the Lord in John iv. that when we worship God in truth we worship Him *as Father* (John iv. 23). For this it is not enough, that we should know that God is our Father. To know that God is our Father is one thing, but *to know the Father* is quite another. It is not a matter of scholarship or attainment, for the veriest babes in the family of God may know the Father (1 John ii. 13). But in order to be acceptable worshippers this knowledge, this holy intimacy is essential. By the gracious teaching and work of the Holy Spirit in our souls, it may be ours.

NEW TESTAMENT PRINCIPLES.

Why is it that expediency and humanly devised regulations are in so many instances allowed to take the place of obedience to the directions as to worship and church procedure laid down in the New Testament ? It is certain that New Testament directions require *New Testament power* if they are to be carried out. Is lack of this the reason ?

The late Alex. Marshall used to relate a conversation that took place in a train between a friend of his and a clergyman. The latter remarked : " I tell my parishioners that they should do about spiritual things as they do about their groceries : go where they are the best served. If the Methodist parson does them more good, let them go to him."

Mr. H. replied that this seemed quite wrong to him. " If what you do is what the Lord commanded, all ought to be there. If contrary to Scripture, neither you nor they have any business there."

" Oh," said the clergyman, " I don't think God has given instructions as to these matters. I believe He leaves us at liberty to do what we consider most suitable, and that we are justified in choosing accordingly."

" On the contrary," replied Mr. H., " I find the Word of God just as explicit about these things as it is about the way of salvation."

" I should very much like you to show me where," said the clergyman.

So they opened their Bibles together in the railway carriage, and turned to one passage after another. They saw how those who gladly received the Gospel were baptized and continued stedfastly in the apostles' doctrine, in fellowship one with another, in the breaking of bread and prayers (Acts ii. 41, 42); how disciples used to come together on the first day of the week to break bread (Acts xx. 7); how that when gathered together all might contribute, one by one, to their mutual edification (1 Corinthians xiv. 31, 32); how elders in each assembly were to feed the flock, looking for their reward when the Chief Shepherd shall appear (1 Peter v. 1-4).

Much more was considered. At last, as the journey was nearing its end, the clergyman said: "I have been deeply interested in all you have said. It is very beautiful indeed as a theory it seems perfect. But it appears to me that in practice it would need some supernatural power to make it work."

"Undoubtedly," replied Mr. H., "that is just what it does need; and *what do you suppose that the Holy Spirit was given for?*"

"Oh," said the clergyman, "I had not thought of that!" Comment upon this is hardly necessary! It is another instance of ignoring the presence of the Holy Spirit and acting as if there were no such Person.

MONTANISTS AND OTHERS.

Again and again, during the history of Christian profession, when the presence and power of the Holy Spirit has been ignored and practically denied by corrupt organizations calling themselves "catholic," "orthodox" or "national" churches, witnesses have been raised up to remind saints of this vital truth.

Amongst these, and very early in the so-called Christian centuries, those known as Montanists arose. The name savours of sectarianism. But, as E. H. Broadbent truly says, " the use of the name of some prominent man to describe an extensive spiritual movement is misleading, and although it must sometimes be accepted for the sake of convenience, it should always be with the reservation that, however important a man may be as a leader and exponent, a spiritual movement affecting multitudes of people is something larger and more significant." In Mr. Broadbent's splendid book, " The Pilgrim Church " (which should be, not on the bookshelf merely, but constantly in the hands of every student of spiritual movements), he describes the rise and testimony of the Montanists as follows :—

" In view of the increasing worldliness in the Church, and the way in which among the leaders learning was taking the place of spiritual power, many believers were deeply impressed with the desire for a fuller experience of the indwelling and power of the Holy Spirit, and were looking for spiritual revival and return to apostolic teaching and practice.

" In Phrygia Montanus began to teach (A.D. 156), he and those with him protesting against the prevailing laxity in the relations of the Church and the world.

" . . . The persecution ordered by the Emperor Marcus Aurelius (A.D. 177) quickened the expectation of the Lord's coming and the spiritual aspirations of the believers. The Montanists hoped to raise up congregations that should return to primitive piety, live as those waiting for the Lord's return and, especially, give to the Holy Spirit His rightful place in the Church. . . . The Catholic system obliged the bishops to take increasing control of the churches, while the Montanists resisted this, maintaining that the guidance of the churches was the prerogative of the Holy Spirit, and that room should be left for His workings.

"These differences soon led to the formation of separate churches in the East. But in the West the Montanists long remained as societies within the Catholic churches, and it was only after many years that they were excluded from, or left, them. In Carthage, Perpetua and Felicitas, the touching record of whose martyrdom has preserved their memory, were still, though Montanists, members of the Catholic church at the time of their martyrdom (A.D. 207), but early in the third century the great leader in the African churches, the eminent writer Tertullian, attaching himself to the Montanists, separated from the Catholic body."

There were regrettable excesses on the part of certain ones among the Montanists. In spite of this, it was evidently a genuine movement towards recovery of the truth of the Holy Spirit's presence. As such it serves as a sample of the many such movements that there have been, and that exist to-day.

THE HOPE OF RIGHTEOUSNESS.

Is not righteousness ours already, by the gift of God ? Is not this what being justified means ? Yes, of course. But in Philippians iii. 9 Paul expresses his ardent desire to be found in Christ, having "the righteousness which is of God by faith." He is thinking forward into the future, when perfection will be reached, and the saints manifested, not only arrayed in a glorious robe of righteousness of God's providing, but as themselves being the expression of how His righteousness had wrought to make them what they are (2 Corinthians v. 21).

When, for any reason, there is declension of soul, or a lending of the ear to erroneous teaching, there is a dimming of this blessed hope. The soul's gaze is diverted to earthborn objects ; the clearness of its vision is blurred.

It was so in the case of the Galatian believers. Taking up with the Law, they had fallen from GRACE. In imagining that they could be justified by Law, they were making Christ " of no effect." But in contrast with the " ye " of whom all this was sadly true, the Apostle says that " WE *through the Spirit* wait for the hope of righteousness by faith " (Galatians v. 5).

Here faith is placed in contrast with Law, and the Spirit in contrast with the flesh, while the " we " who stand fast in Christian liberty are in contrast with the " ye " who were allowing themselves to be misled by teachers of the Law. They had begun in the Spirit, but it seemed as if now they sought perfection by the flesh (Galatians iii. 3). Says Paul, as it were : " *We* are not like that. *We* are of the principle of faith, not of Law. *We* walk in the Spirit, not in the flesh. And by the Spirit *we* are actuated by a glorious hope."

The Holy Spirit turns our thoughts to the future. We are " saved in hope " (Romans viii. 24, R.V.) ; that is, we are saved in view of something that yet lies ahead. We have fled to Christ for refuge to lay hold of this sure and certain hope, which already connects us with what is " within the veil " (Hebrews vi. 19). It is a hope laid up for us in heaven (Colossians i. 5). It disconnects our thoughts, our aims, our plans, our outlook from earth and links them with heaven.

Into all that this glorious hope implies and includes we shall be brought at the coming of the Lord. In view of this " the Spirit and the Bride say, Come " (Revelation xxii. 17). The Holy Spirit begets in our hearts bridal affections for our coming Bridegroom, and leads us to join in the appeal to Him to come. He keeps this hope alive within our breasts, and thus it is by the Spirit that we " wait for the hope of righteousness."

THE SPIRIT OF JESUS.

There is no doubt whatever that the true reading of the last clause of Acts xvi. 7 is : " the Spirit of Jesus suffered them not." The R.V. or any recent translation will assure the English reader of this. The phrase is an unusual one, and it is well that we should enquire why He who is called in verse 6 " the Holy Spirit " should in verse 7 be called " the Spirit of Jesus."

It was in view of the evangelization of the great heathen continent of Europe that the Spirit of Jesus would not allow Paul, Silas and Timothy to go to the Asiatic province of Bithynia. The title seems intended to remind us of the truly evangelistic heart of the Lord Jesus when on earth.

Early in His ministry He so preached the Gospel that in Judaea He " made and baptised more disciples than John " (John iv. 1). We have no record of this tremendous campaign, truly amazing for the scale of its success, though apparently Peter refers to it when he says that the word which God sent, preaching peace by Jesus Christ, " was published throughout all Judaea " (Acts x. 37).

John alone tells us of the Lord's visit to Samaria. He spent two days in that province, winning many of the Samaritans to faith in Himself as the Saviour of the world (John iv. 41, 42).

It is Mark who gives us the most vivid insight into the gracious activities of the Lord, as He constantly thought of " the regions beyond." In the first ten chapters of his Gospel he mentions nine distinct campaigns :

1. Throughout the whole of the northern province : i. 39 and on.
2. The country of the Gerasenes (R.V.) : v. 1 and on.

3. A return visit to the villages of Galilee : vi. 6.
4. The land of Gennesaret ; its villages, cities and countryside : vi. 53-56.
5. The territory of Tyre and Sidon : vii. 24-30.
6. The territory of Decapolis : vii. 31-viii. 9.
7. The district of Dalmanutha : viii. 10-26.
8. The towns of Caesarea Philippi : viii. 27 and on.
9. The Trans-Jordan territory of Judaea : x. 1-16.

Even to the very end just prior to the Crucifixion, the Saviour was found in the Temple, not only teaching the people, but preaching the Gospel (Luke xx. 4).

The Holy Spirit, as the Spirit of Jesus, closed doors in the East in order to lead the servants of Christ westward to Europe. It was, may we not say, the Spirit of Jesus that gave Paul the intention of passing by Rome (where his ministry was greatly needed) to go to Spain (Romans xv. 28). To-day the Spirit of Jesus leads preachers of the Word to India, China, Africa and the islands of far-off seas. But great territories in Europe are to-day without witnesses for Christ, and He who bade His disciples look on the Samaritan fields, white unto harvest, may yet bid servants of His look on Latvian, Lithuanian, Hungarian, Rumanian, Polish and Bulgarian fields, and the Spirit of Jesus may move labourers to go thither.

FIRST AND LAST MENTIONS.

To put together the first reference to any subject in Scripture and the last is often very helpful. I think we shall find this to be the case in connection with the Holy Spirit.

The first mention of Him, in Genesis i. 2, pictures Him moving with His divine energy to give effect to the Word by which all created things were brought into existence. With omniscient foresight He wrought in those primeval days to prepare the arena where afterwards such wonderful deeds would be performed, and where eventually the Son of God would suffer and die. He, the Spirit, was the mighty power by which God would work in the world that was then in the making, to bring His own gracious and eternal designs to pass.

When we come to the last mention of the Holy Spirit, in Revelation xxii. 17, we are approaching the consummation of the divine purposes. John had (in vision) been rapt away by the Spirit into a wilderness to view the destruction of the counterfeit bride, "the great whore" (Revelation xvii. 3). After this, he is again rapt away in his vision by the Spirit to a high mountain (xxi. 10) where he gets a sight of the true Bride, the holy Jerusalem, descending from heaven to take her place during the years of the millennial kingdom with her heavenly Bridegroom. The previous verses (1 to 3) give a view of her in the eternal state, where both the heavens and the earth are new. Then the vision goes back to times when there would yet be nations and kings (verse 24). The light in which they walk, the guidance that they receive, will not come from angels, but from the city which is the Bride of the Lamb.

Before any of this can come to pass the Bridegroom Himself must come. He presents Himself as the coming One, the Bright and Morning Star, and immediately the Spirit gives utterance to the response of every loyal and loving heart. He, with the Bride, replies "Come." And the last petition that He indites is again in response to the word "Surely I come quickly." It is this : " Even so, come, Lord Jesus" (xxii. 20). Happy are they who can join in this cry with their whole hearts.

THE BENEDICTION.

" The grace of the Lord Jesus Christ, and the love of God, and the communion of the Holy Ghost, be with you all. Amen " (2 Corinthians xiii. 14).

How familiar the words are ! The very fact of their familiarity, it is to be feared, sometimes robs them of their significance. In the mouths of some they become a mere formula of dismissal, uttered as a matter of routine and heard without thought or exercise on the part of many.

It is a thousand pities that this should be so, for the sacred words have a tremendous import. The verse is one of the few where all the three Persons of the Triune Godhead are named, the Holy Spirit being God equally with the Father and the Son. Not three Gods in one Person, but one God existing in three Persons.

" *The grace of the Lord Jesus Christ* " was shown in the past by His becoming poor for our sakes (2 Corinthians viii. 9). It is not, however, confined to that, as if it were a mere matter of history. It is warm, tender and true to-day, and the prayer of the Benediction is that it may be with us, that is, that we may have the reality of it, and the consciousness of it, wherever we go.

" *The love of God.*" This also was convincingly manifested in the past in the gift of His Son. " In this was manifested the love of God toward us, because that God sent His only begotten Son into the world, that we might live through Him " (1 John iv. 9). But it also is a present reality. It is a love that holds us in its eternal embrace. Nothing can separate us from it.

" *The communion of the Holy Ghost.*" The meaning of this is not quite so evident as that of the preceding words. It carries with it, of course, the thought of communion with the Father and the Son in which we share through the ministry of the apostles, to whom it first pertained (1 John i. 3). But it most assuredly conveys also the thought of communion one with another. It is what we cometimes pray for in the words of a familiar hymn :

> " Thus may ours be sweet communion
> With each other and the Lord."

It means the putting away all that would introduce a discordant note, all envy, suspicion, evil speaking, uncharitable thoughts, divisions, selfishness, etc.

This is what is implied in " the communion of the Holy Ghost." Strife and discord among Christians are works of *the flesh* (Galatians v. 20), whereas the fruit of the Spirit is " love, joy, peace " (verse 22). The Spirit of God, the God of peace, works for practical unity, love and mutual forbearance among His saints. When we pray : " the communion of the Holy Ghost be with you all," we are praying that we may all be kept in the current of His working, never making a contribution to the enemy's evil work of fostering discord and strife, but that we may be preserved in harmony, in that communion which is of the Holy Spirit's making.

A WARNING.

" Now if any man have not the Spirit of Christ, he is none of His " (Romans viii. 9).

In this verse " the Spirit of Christ " does not mean Christlikeness. It means the Holy Spirit, who is described in this chapter in so many different terms : " the Spirit of Him that raised up Jesus from the dead "; " the Spirit of God "; " the Spirit of sonship "; " the Spirit of life in Christ Jesus."

" All believers have the Holy Ghost. ' If any man have not the Spirit of Christ '—that is, the Third Person of the Blessed Trinity, not the disposition or mind of Christ merely—' he is none of His.' This is the grand distinctive mark of all God's children."

So wrote the late Evan H. Hopkins, and we believe he was right. But erroneous teaching is given in some quarters on these lines : " You may be a true believer, yet you may not have received the Holy Spirit. There may be no fruit in your life, no evidence of His indwelling, no sorrow for sin, no sincere self-judgment, no effort to please and serve Him, no love for His people. You may be just living for self, to have ' a good time.' You have not received the Holy Spirit. Yet of course, if you once believed in Christ you belong to Him, and are saved for ever."

Thus worldly minded people, whose whole lives give the lie to the assumption that they belong to Christ, are persuaded that, after all, because they once "believed," they are on their way to heaven !

What I should like to say to any such worldling is this : " Do not delude yourself with the idea that you are a real Christian. It is manifest from your life, your outlook, your selfishness, your whole course in the world, that you are not indwelt by the Holy Spirit. This does not mean that you are a kind of lower grade believer. It means that you are not a genuine believer at all. You may believe like Simon in Acts viii. 13 ; that is, you may give credence to the facts which the Gospel sets forth, without repentance. Like Simon, though believing after this fashion and perhaps baptized, as he was, you have neither part nor lot in vital Christianity. Your heart is not right in the sight of God. You are still in the bond of iniquity. Never having received the Holy Spirit, you do not belong to Christ at all. You are *none of His*."

If we have received the Holy Spirit, there will assuredly be some evidence of it in our lives. We shall have our " fruit unto holiness " (Romans vi. 22). Where this is lacking we shall deceive ourselves if we imagine that our feet are on the road to heaven. *Without holiness no man shall see the Lord* (Hebrews xii. 14).

THE HOLY SPIRIT Here Today

Reference	Page
Genesis i. 2	101, 171
i. 3, 6	32
vi. 3	61, 102, 103
viii. 6—12	92
xxiv.	83 85 86 89
Exodus xvi. 13, 14	94
Leviticus ii. 6, 11	96
xiv. 14, 17	27
xxii. 10, 11	28
xxiv. 16	129
xxvii. 10	105
Numbers xi. 9	94
xix.	97 98
xxi. 6—18	98
xxiv. 2	53 134
Deuteronomy vii. 7	145
Judges vi. 34	80
Ruth ii. 5	89
I Samuel iii. 19	83
x. 1	160
x. 10	134
x. 6, 7, 10	53
xvi. 13	160
1 Kings xx. 27	145
Ezra i. 5	145
ix. 8	145
Esther iv. 16	136
Job xxvii. 13	102
xxxvi. 7	34
Psalm xlv. 6	45
xxiv. 5	150
xl. 5	138
li. 7	97
xcv.	105
cv. 27	54
cxxxix. 17	138
Isaiah i. 9	145
iv. 4, 5, 6	108 109
Jeremiah xxxi. 33, 34	119
Ezekiel xl. 4, 5, 45, 46	88
xliii. 10	89
xlvii. 5	89
Daniel ix. 21	88
x. 8, 17, 18, 19	138 139
Hosea xiv. 1, 2, 3, 4	66
Joel ii. 19—28	93
ii. 28	109
ii. 28—31	54
Amos ii. 10	50 51
Micah ii. 8	109
Haggai ii. 3	145
Zechariah iv. 1—6	109
iv. 10	144
Malachi iv. 2	146
Matthew i. 20	96
i. 23	18
iii. 11	45 46 47
iii. 7—12	47
xi. 5	106
xiii. 33	96
xiii. 51	105
xiv. 12	112
xxii. 1—14	92
xxv. 8	134
xxvii. 62—66	34
Mark i. 8	46
i. 39	170
iii. 28—30	61 129
v. 1	170
vi. 6	171
vi. 13	46
vi. 53—56	171
viii. 24—30, 31e	171
viii. 10—86, 27e	171
x. 1—16	171
Luke i. 15, 41, 67	45 81
i. 35	96
iii. 16	46
viii. 13	135
ix. 6	46
x. 17	46
xi. 13	23
xii. 46	134
xiv. 16—23	91
xiv. 23	107
xx. 4	171
xxiv. 49	41
John i. 32	82
i. 33	46
John ii.	78

INDEX OF TEXTS.

John iii. 3, 6	28
ii. 5, 6	45
iii. 5, 8	31
iii. 6	107
iv. 1	170
iv. 14	31 99
iv. 23	164
iv. 41, 42	170
v. 21	106
vi. 27	33
vi. 47	133
vii. 38	31 98
vii. 39	22
x. 28	133
xi. 4, 25	106
xiv. 13	59
xiv. 16	17 20 54 56 62
xiv. 17	21 22 27 149
xiv. 26	17 20 59
xv. 26	19 56 83
xvi. 7	23
xvi. 7—12	56
xvi. 8, 9	149
xvi. 13	19 58
xvi. 14	17 19
Acts i. 2	128
i. 4	52
i. 5	45 46
i. 8	41 108
i. 14	23
i. 16	104
ii. 1	69
ii. 1—4	38 39 40
ii. 4	43
ii. 11	43
ii. 33	52
ii. 38	25
ii. 41, 42	166
iv. 8	45 81
iv. 31	71
iv. 33	147
v. 3	71 130
v. 32	24
vi. 3	81
vii. 51	60
viii. 1	148
Acts viii. 3	149
viii. 13	175
viii. 14—17	42
viii. 15—17	110
viii. 29	80
ix. 17	45
ix. 31	57 128
x. 11	146
x. 37	96 170
x. 43	18 36
x. 44	110
x. 44—46	42
x. 45	52
xi. 15	52
xi. 16	52
xi. 24	81
xiii. 4	90
xiii. 9	81
xiii. 38—39	116
xiii. 39	133
xiii. 55	81 110
xiv. 1	146
xv. 3	149
xvi. 6, 7	90 170
xvi.	170
xvi. 25	163
xvii. 10, 11	114
xviii. 8	49
xix. 1—8	111
xix. 6	42
xx. 7	69 166
xxii. 6	146
xxvi. 11	129
xxvi. 13	146
xxviii. 25	50
Romans i. 4	106 122
i. 17	108
i. 24, 26, 28	103
iii. 22	108
iv. 5	108
v. 1, 2	122 123
v. 5	35 108
vi. 10, 11	140 141
vi. 22	176
vii. 24	140
viii. 2	140

INDEX OF TEXTS.

Reference	Pages
Rom. viii. 9	134 174
viii. 11	21 45 127
viii. 15	142
viii. 16	122 124
viii. 23	36
viii. 24	169
xv. 28	171
xvi. 20	162
1 Corinthians i. 11, 12	49
i. 13, 17, 18, 23	143
ii. 2 4 8 10 11 12 13 14	88 143 144
ii. 10	88
iii. 3	43 49
iii. 17	72
vi. 6, 11	49
vi. 19	18 21 125 127
x. 1, 2	50
xi. 21, 22	49
xii. 13	45 48
xii. 12—27	49
xii. 30	43
xiii. 8	43
xiv. 1, 5, 6, 14—19, 22	43
xiv. 2—28, 39	43
xiv. 23	69 70
xiv. 31, 32	166
2 Corinthians i. 21	45 160
i. 22	24 32 45 72
v. 5	72 73
v. 11	91
v. 21	168
viii. 9	173
xiii. 3—5	117
xiii. 14	173
Galatians iii. 3	169
iii. 27	30
iv. 6	25 142
iv. 19	30
v. 5	2 169
v. 20, 22	174
Gal. v. 22, 23	139
Ephesians i. 13	35 45 125
i. 14	45 72 73
ii. 5	128
ii. 18	135
ii. 22	137
Eph. iii. 16	138
iv. 3	40
iv. 4	100
iv. 30	19 36 45 60 62
iv. 32	24
v. 18	45 53 76 81
v. 26	31
v. 27	87
vi. 18	25
Philippians i. 9—11	139
iii. 3	163
iii. 9	168
iii. 21	128
Colossians i. 5	169
i. 12	24
i. 27	140
iii. 2, 8, 12	140
iii. 16	81
1 Thessalonians iv. 8	25
v. 19	60 70
v. 20	70
2 Thessalonians ii. 7, 8	48
1 Timothy i. 13	129
2 Timothy i. 7	147
i. 14	21 45
Hebrews i. 7	52
iv. 12	105
vi. 4—6	132 133 135
vi. 19	169
ix ; x.	119
x. 2	121
x. 3	119
x. 5	18 48
x. 14, 15	109
x. 15, 16	107 117
x. 17	107 117 122
x. 27	48
x. 29	107
xi. 19	84
Heb. xii. 14	176
James i. 18	31
ii. 8	160
v. 16	75
1 Peter i. 11	104
i. 12	104 107
i. 23, 25	31

INDEX OF TEXTS.

1 Peter ii. 9	160
iv. 10	147
iv. 14	162
v. 1—4	166
v. 10	147
2 Peter i. 21	104
1 John i. 3	174
ii. 13	164
ii 20	160 161
ii. 27	45 160 161
iii. 24	25
iv. 9	173
iv. 16	137
1 John v. 6—13,	124
v. 16	131
Jude 3	59
11	53
Jude 14, 15	104
20	25
Revelation i. 1	60
i. 4	100 101
i. 10	100
ii. 14	53
iii. 1	101
iii. 14	107
iv. 5	101
v. 6	101
xi. 4	109
xvii. 3	172
xxi. 1—3, 10	172
xxi. 3	137
xxii. 16	84
xxii. 17	100 169 172
xxii. 20	172